PRAISE FOR LIZ SCHEID'S
THE SHAPE OF BLUE

"From the fabric of her own life, Liz Scheid creates an intricate tapestry that explores how we might cope with our fragile human situation, the chronic ache of separation and connectedness—of gathering and loss. 'I feel as though I've been propelled inward,' she writes at one point, and so does the reader, encountering Scheid's overlapping worlds of imagination, memory, consciousness and scientific fact. This is a beautiful, brilliant book, clear and compelling—and profoundly moving."

—Corrinne Clegg Hales, author of
To Make It Right

"Family is one thread in *The Shape of Blue*, but the book also deftly handles the intersection of birth and death, presence and absence. Scheid weaves 'silver and beautiful' associations that keenly depict the angles we use to navigate life in an exciting new collection that combines the lyric and the familiar."

—Carmen Gimenez Smith, author of
Bring Down the Little Birds

"*The Shape of Blue* is a stunning literary debut, a book that is both haunted and heroic; a masterful blend of science writing and lyrical, luminous personal reflection on fear and family, love and loss, and the sublime interstices between the things of this world. To read this book is to feel deliciously lost in language and fact, consistently surprised, even heartbroken at the emotional depths it reaches. Readers who appreciate the writing of Lia Purpura, Amy Leach, or Maggie Nelson will love Liz Scheid's *The Shape of Blue*."

—Steven Church, author of
The Day After The Day After: My Atomic Angst

"A tender prose poem eulogy to her sister who died in a car accident, Liz Scheid's *The Shape of Blue* explores death, grief, motherhood and anxiety with tender lyricism. With arresting imagery, she forges beautiful connections between snowflakes, EKGs, astronomy, paleontology and language. A deep and stunning book."

—Marie Carter, author of
The Trapeze Diaries

the SHAPE of BLUE

NOTES ON LOSS, LANGUAGE, MOTHERHOOD & FEAR

LIZ SCHEID

LIT PUB
BOOKS
thelitpub.com

Cover art and design by Jana Vukovic.
Prepress by sunnyoutside.
Copy edited by Sheila McMullin.

ISBN: 978-1-937662-09-7

Thank you to the editors of the following magazines for publishing these pieces, some in their very early or beginning stages: *Juked:* "Ten Years After," formerly "A Cemetery At Night In December, Ten Years After"; *Mississippi Review:* "Jellyfish"; *Sou'Wester:* "Door Collecting"; *Terrain:* "How It Begins," formerly "It Begins In Neon Lights"; *The Journal:* "What Is The Shape"; *The Rumpus:* "The End Of A World As We Know It."

for
Bret, Amaya, and Anderson

"You become what you think about all day long."
—Ralph Waldo Emerson

CONTENTS

the SHAPE of BLUE

WHAT IS THE SHAPE

OF DISTANCE

I've been staring at the linea nigra, a bluish jagged line that connects my pelvis to belly button. At 34 weeks pregnant with my second baby, my body is scattered with blue shapes: spider veins burst along calves like webs, veins on wrists wrap around each other in deep purple lines. I don't recognize my body. My feet look detached from legs, like two swollen entities. I trace the line separating me from my baby.

The distance between California and Wisconsin is roughly 1,800 miles. Give or take. As a child, I flew back and forth from California to Wisconsin several times a year, bouncing between states, between parents. After the divorce, my dad moved back to Wisconsin, where we started. My head pressed against the plane window as I watched the horizon collapse. I like being in flight. Time seems suspended in the sky.

OF TIME

During pregnancy, time moves backward. Like back-stroking through a dream. Things you think you know vanish—or the thought hangs in the backdrop and you can't pinpoint the word for it. Like trying to put your hand on static in the air.

In 1962, George Kubler's book, *The Shape of Time,* was released. Among other things, Kubler suggested that strings of events, which follow each other at different speeds, shape time.

During pregnancy, short-term memory disappears. In the morning, I lose my cups of tea. They seem to sink into a black hole. I make more, and later in the day I find cold cups of tea in closets, on bookshelves, atop dressers. My mind moves in a flurry.

My sister Sarah gave birth to her second child by C-section. For days after, the incision burned, slicing into skin. Her belly looked swollen and sore. She was supposed to rest. Doctors told her to stay in bed. Stubborn and driven, she lifted and bent, moved in ways she shouldn't have. She had a three-year-old and a newborn. She tried to fight time, to move against what was pushing her back. Three months later, she died in a car accident.

OF ANGER

In Wisconsin, my dad rented a cottage across the street from a lake. I spent summers with him, where the warm rain feels like soup. While he worked, I spent most days with a friend by the lake. We swam under the long silver pier where the water was cooler. If a fish tickled our toes, we emerged from the water, disgusted. When Dad came home, he would cook dinner, and then we would watch a movie or play basketball. Some nights, after talking to my mom on the telephone, he asked if I wanted to go for a drive. During those long rides through back roads, he said nothing. We listened to music, watching rows and rows of corn swirl past. It seemed his anger was suspended in his voice box.

These last few days, my baby has been kicking my ribs rapidly. His agitation follows these triggers: loud voices, caffeine, my lying too still.

OF WATER

My mom loved California's hot weather. She was tired of long, cold winters in Wisconsin. She said her skin looked gray there, her hair like ash. She wanted more color, more sun, more time out of the house. She wanted to be closer to her family. In those days I saw her as my mother/mom/mama/nurturer/caretaker. I couldn't understand she had other needs. When she gathered us all into the living room to tell us we were moving to Fresno, I was afraid but also excited. I had never been to California, but I imagined a massive ocean with sandy beaches and seashells. I saw it as an adventure, but my siblings weren't happy. They were afraid of the change, afraid to leave friends and familiarity. We rented a house with a black bottom pool and spent hot days floating on rafts, tipping each other over. Mom seemed to come alive again after we moved—her demeanor changed. I liked seeing her so happy. Some nights, we swam and blared the music.

Dad loved to fish, and he complained about the "man-made" lakes in the San Joaquin Valley. He called them mud holes. Early mornings in Wisconsin, when we were young, he used to take my brother and sisters and me to the lake three blocks away. He showed us how to cast a line. I didn't have much patience. All I wanted was to swim. To keep me in the boat, Sarah told me there were piranhas in cages at the bottom of the lake, and if my feet got too close they would bite off my toes.

At this point in the pregnancy, my amniotic fluid is at its highest peak. He is swimming in it, digesting and excreting it. His muscles and bones move at ease in this watered cocoon.

OF SCARS

Sarah had a beautiful blue scar on her elbow. When we were kids, she fell out of our brother's tree fort and ran inside, hysterical, to show Mom, who nearly fainted when she saw the white bone in all that blood. Sarah was in the hospital for what felt like weeks. I just wanted her to come home. We visited every day, and I was jealous of all the attention she got—all of her yogurt and ice cream and balloons. Her elbow was shattered in pieces, and her wrist was broken. Surgeons had to use pins to piece the bones together. During surgery, a pin slipped and they almost had to amputate her arm. They managed to salvage it, but afterward she couldn't straighten her arm all the way, and her sharp elbow protruded. She was always showing off her scar to a group of big-eyed neighbor boys, making them swoon with jealousy, which reinforced her wild girl/tomboy ways.

I have a scar on my mouth. The tissue runs thick inside, making it hard to pull that skin. I don't remember the incident. I know the stories passed on to me by my parents and siblings. I've heard so many different versions that I imagine the truth to be a collision of them all—somewhere within the gray territory. I do know this: I bit an electrical cord. It was an old fan. Heather, five at the time, yanked the cord from my mouth. Doctors said it is amazing she didn't also receive the shock. My great-grandma was watching us. Mom told me that she and Dad cried when they first saw my mouth, that my face looked battered, swollen, and the corner looked like a burnt marshmallow. There was also a blister on the bottom of my foot, where the electricity that surged through my small body left me. I also know I would have died had Heather not pulled the cord. I don't know why but when I try to reimagine this day, I wonder where Sarah was. Or my brother. Were they outside? What did my great-grandma do when my sister must have come running down the stairs to tell her I was burned? Did she say I was on fire? At five, she couldn't have known the word: *electrocuted*. Or maybe she did. Maybe that's what she yelled from the third floor of our house. Such ruminations only produce more questions, more speculation and wonder. What I have left is a jagged scar. It defines me in many ways. Every time I see an uncle or aunt I haven't seen for a while, their eyes zoom in on it as they shake their heads and tell me if I only knew what a miracle it is that I'm alive. At one time, I considered plastic surgery. I saw my scar as a flaw, a deformity. Now I can't imagine my mouth without it. Everything I say filters through.

OF DREAMS

My dad had the same dream several nights in a row: he's fishing, everything begins to ascend into the air—silver fish, shadows of other fishermen, snakes—and as he begins to rise in his boat, he stops midway. Everything else rises past him as his boat hovers halfway up into the sky. When he tells me about this dream, I listen closely because usually he keeps his feelings and emotions to himself.

Amaya tells me she dreamed about yellow hummingbirds. Everywhere. She was so small, she could ride them.

During pregnancy, I dream a lot about my sister. At some point in every dream, I realize it isn't real, that I'm dreaming, that she's dead, and I ask her what she's doing here. She never answers, and then I wake up and everything feels distorted again. Like she keeps dying over and over.

OF BRUISES

At first, my parents thought they wanted an open casket. They thought it might bring closure. It never felt
like any of us were making any conscious decisions in
the immediate days after her death. I remember clutch-
ing Mom's arm as we all walked down the stairs of the
morgue. No one wanted to look at the shiny caskets on
display. We didn't move forward. I think we picked the
one closest to where we were standing. It was silver and
engraved with roses. There's something disconcerting
about standing in a basement with open caskets on display—you can't help but think of your own mortality or
your own stiff body inside. When someone so close to
you dies so suddenly, you obsess so much more.

There is no way to prepare yourself for viewing a loved
one's body in the casket you helped pick. Mom fell on
the floor beside her, folding her head into her lap, saying, "This isn't her. She's not here." Dad walked in, held
his breath and all his emotion, and walked out. I'm not
sure if I ever saw him exhale. I stood back for a while, in
Bret's embrace. I wanted to see Sarah's hands because
mine were eerily similar—long skinny fingers, inherited from Mom's side. Music teachers used to beg us to
play the piano. I've been warned by doctors about ar-
thritis. Someone had folded hers like a paper fan. There
was a yellow bruise between her left thumb and index
finger. I stared hard, losing myself in its shape, wondering how she got it. She must have been gripping the
steering wheel when her car flipped. When did she let
go? I have obsessed about *when* she let go, *how* she let
go, a million times over, *what* song was playing on the

radio, *what* was the last image she saw. If you tell yourself to stop thinking morbid thoughts, you think them all the more.

Lately, my body bruises easily. All the pressure on veins and lack of iron. Amaya traces a small bruise on my arm with her finger. She tells me it's shaped like a heart and asks if I know that all bruises are blue hearts.

OF LOSS

Shortly before the divorce, my parents went on a retreat to try to reconcile. There was a distance between them, and Mom said they had trouble communicating. Silence is the worst kind of anger because it drowns out all other sounds. The retreat was in the mountains, and they took walks up hills, up paths with overgrown flowers and weeds, and they rested on rocks. Dad wrote her a beautiful letter with beautiful words. She said it was long and heartfelt, and she never knew he felt so strongly. She says she touched each word with her finger. It's almost as though they did this subconsciously to make peace before letting each other go. I know there's so much more to their story I'll never learn, not just because of what they don't share but because it belongs to them.

The semester she died, Sarah was enrolled in a nursing program. We tried to convince her to slow down, take the semester off, but she was determined to move forward. She had a vision, a goal, and she wasn't about to let her pregnancy deter her. She felt guilty because she had her first son so young, causing her to postpone college for a period. Now that he was in preschool, she was motivated to finish her degree. I scheduled my own classes around hers, so I could watch my nephews for her. I remember seeing her in blue scrubs in those early mornings with her cup of coffee in hand. She looked so beautiful, professional, happy. I use this word sparingly, but she was *happy*. She had always been more domestic than I was, but she was so much more than an amazing mother. She was a *smart* woman. She was far more hands-on than I'll ever be. She could take things apart, put things back together. Whenever I would get a new dresser or shelf, I would have her put it together. Maybe that's why she chose nursing. It embodied the best of both worlds: intellect and physicality. I hated blood. She wasn't afraid of it. I wanted to be fearless like her. She convinced me to take an evening class with her that semester: The Psychology of Crime. It was everything it suggests: disturbing, mind-blowing, alluring. We became obsessed with serial killers: Charles Manson, Ted Bundy, Jeffrey Dahmer. We shared the desire, the obsession even, to know how and why someone could be driven to that kind of madness. At the end of the semester, we worked hard on our research papers, calling each other late at night to find out what page each one of us was on. I proofread hers. We turned ours in together, but she never saw her final score. She died a week after she turned it in. The professor of the course came to the wake, offered his condolences and handed me her graded essay: "I graded this before she died. I thought you should know. It was a great paper. I thought you should have it." His eyes were red. I save her paper in a blue box of other treasures I've kept: letters, perfume, lotion, pictures, notebooks. I trace my finger over her blue-inked words and doodles, glimpsing how her mind moved in those present seconds and feel like I'm with her again.

On Sundays, my dad fishes in the early mornings. He anchors his boat in the most secluded spot, just above all the weeds. I've been with him—and it's beautiful—the boat's hum, whistling cicadas, black lake, distant porch lights. The shaping of a day. Like you're sitting inside a pool of loss. There are no words. It encircles you, and everything feels watered. Like the mind during pregnancy. You tell yourself to move forward. Something pulls you back.

THE END OF A WORLD
AS WE KNOW IT

My obsession with Pluto began when my six-year-old daughter asked how many planets there were. Nine. Nine! Nine? There had always been nine, and I couldn't bring myself to say "eight."

In 2006, when the International Astronomical Union (IAU) announced to the world that Pluto was no longer a planet, it felt like the end times, a projection of the doom impending: apocalyptic floods, the walloping of a clandestine planet, a searing irate sun, continents throwing us overboard. Why the drama?

I wanted to understand why I was having such a visceral reaction to the demotion, so I began searching for answers. Why would they do such a thing?

I immersed myself in research, seduced by the language surrounding Pluto: *this cold planet in a tilted orbit.*

Orbit. A path an object embarks on as the result of centripetal force pulling it to its center of rotation. Most orbits are elliptical. As in: *you spin me right around baby, right around.* An elliptical orbit is more oval, more like an ellipse—an absence, a closed curve. What's left unsaid, a suggestion of more, less. . . .

Pluto always sort of hung off the edge of the world. It was the Boho planet, the way it collapsed categories. Its elusiveness was appealing. I could relate to its quirkiness, having never really fit in myself. When I was in elementary school, my parents were concerned about my preference for imaginary friends over neighbor kids, or how I named and talked to inanimate objects, like toothbrushes. I lived in my head, creating stories. My teacher told my parents they should seek help for me if I never escaped my head. That is, if I could not distinguish reality from fantasy.

To many, Pluto was a period, a symbol of security, an ending. We trusted our limits because the illusion was time, was linear, after all. We begin, we end. Hello (*I love you*), goodbye (*this is the end*). There's comfort in this, security. The unknown is dangerous, threatening.

But for me it was the opposite, reality was dangerous. I felt safer in my imaginary world. I scratched stories and poems into notebooks, rereading and rewriting worlds. In my imaginary one, I was in control of outcomes.

I think of William Carlos Williams: "No ideas but in things."

The problem is Pluto was more than an abstraction. We saw it in books, named it, attached ourselves to it, plastered it on our ceilings and named our dogs after it. We all know the rule: if we name it, we become attached. "It" becomes *something* with a face, an identity, a soul. Pluto was a distinction that offered a sense of permanence. Words seem stable enough.

My husband and I have been teaching our two-year-old son the words for objects: *moon, sunflower, avocado*. I walk him through the garden: *tomato, vine, earthworm, green onion*. I am teaching myself the scientific names of plants, mostly because I like the sound: *Tulbaghia, Buddleja, Chrysanthemum*. This is how we navigate—

Words. Words. Words.

They are sign posts. Our compass for unknown territory.

Yes, I tell my composition students often, words matter. Each word must have a purpose, a function. Watch what you say. Words can conjure up baggage, history, meaning, emotions, power. . . .

At least for me, words were very powerful. They had the magic to bend time, collapse boundaries.

.   •   .

Recently, we took the kids to the Griffith Observatory in Pasadena, California. The observatory sits at the top of a mountain, closer to the brilliant sky. Inside the dome, I felt like I was walking through tunnels of intertwined minds. I read closely each exhibit's caption, trying to trace the beginnings. I learned how the "eye" was the most important astronomical instrument in the early days of discovery. These early observers sketched drawings and detailed notes describing the positions, movements, and brightness of objects in the sky. They called these dots "planets," meaning "wanderers." To "wander" is to roam. Is to drift. Is to hover. Is to stray. I wondered how they could name something so transient. These early flecks of light were named after Roman deities: Jupiter, king of gods; Mars, god of war; Mercury, messenger of the gods; Venus, goddess of love and beauty; Saturn, father of Jupiter and god of agriculture. These wanderers were seen as otherworldly, heavenly, drifting around a static Earth.

It was Nicholas Copernicus, inventor of the solar system, who declared the sun the center, surrounded by six planets: Mercury, Venus, Earth (with moon), Mars, Jupiter, Saturn. As centuries piled on, the system grew more complex. Uranus was seen through a telescope in 1781, even though it had been spotted at least six times before but mistaken as a star because of its slow movement. I was fascinated with their minds and obsession for answers. One of the exhibits displayed replicas of Galileo's telescope made of wood and leather. It wasn't the first telescope, but his version enhanced observing power to eight-times magnification. With the invention of the telescope, planets were popping up everywhere: Ceres, Astraea, Flora, Hygeia, Kalliope. And in 1846, Neptune emerged: a beautiful blue balloon. By 1854, there were 41 planets! But the planets were supposed to be ethereal, distinct. It seemed fair that the biggest survived as planets. After all, people might get overwhelmed. Too many planets meant too many distinctions. How could they possibly remember so much? The smaller ones were to slip into minor categories/subtypes/subsections, below the norm, below the surface. Almost, but not quite. See also the subconscious. The planet criterion was still broad, blurry, and when Pluto surfaced, it pushed boundaries. . . .

Helen Keller: "When I learned the meaning of 'I' and 'me' and found that I was something, I began to think. Then consciousness first existed for me."

. . .

Going back again. After German astronomer Johann Gottfried Galle discovered Neptune in 1846, astronomers realized it didn't move in its orbit as predicted. Speculations emerged that there was an unseen object introducing "gravitational perturbations" in the planet's orbit. As in: some other force, some other misshapen body. Or what scientists called "Planet X." Or later "Pluto." The origins of Pluto are as murky and multilayered as the mind. Many attribute the discovery of Pluto to American astronomer Percival Lowell, who had a promising career as diplomat but shifted careers and decided to pursue his passion in astronomy, which came in part from possibilities on Mars. I love him for losing himself in his passion.

In 1878, Italian astronomer Giovanni Schiaparelli published a memoir of his observations on Mars: a detailed map of the northern hemisphere, showing islands and peninsulas divided by blue bands of water, which he labeled "curtail"—Italian for "channels." Soon after, these terms were mistranslated in the English-speaking world as "canals." Lowell loved this, became obsessed with the canals of Mars. He insisted that the canals were indicative of intelligent life on Mars. He produced his own detailed maps with more canals. He swore that Mars was growing excessively dry as a result of "planetary evolution." He visualized inhabitants pumping water from poles to desert-like populated areas near the equator. He said: "The amazing blue network on Mars hints that one planet besides our own is inhabited now." His observations are so beautiful, I want to believe them to make them real. He was more storyteller than scientist. More dreamer than realist. He drifted in wonder, meandered in shaded skies. He built his own observatory in Flagstaff, Arizona, 7,200 feet above sea level, staring into black space, where boundaries didn't matter and dream and reality merged. He publicized his findings in magazine articles and wrote three books on the subject. Somewhere along the way, his visions became more than stories, more than observations. They became factual, so much so that he had a mental breakdown in 1897 after scientists refused to believe his theories. Imagine a mind that can travel that far and not be taken seriously.

I used to hide all of my notebooks filled with endless lists of names and stories under my bed. I was terrified of losing these or of someone finding them and disregarding them as silly, childish, strange, or make-believe. I was afraid of being misunderstood.

Lowell continued to spiral downward: in 1907, astronomers released photographs that showed no sign of canals. They concluded these to be an optical illusion.

After this, he took his mental break. Four years later, he emerged to observe, even more determined than before, as if he had been asleep all that time. He widened his obsession to include Mars, Venus, Mercury, and Saturn. He hired more staff. One of his assistants, Vesto Melvin Slipher, made an important discovery about "spiral nebulae." It moved away from Earth. Which was the first evidence of Earth expanding. He also initiated the search for Planet X beyond Neptune's orbit. His fixation shifted to capturing an image of this mysterious planet that he knew was there. He photographed the wide sky week after week, night after night, studying each image. But he always came up empty-handed. However, years later, after his death, it was found Lowell did actually discover an image of Pluto on film, but its presence eluded his assistants. That is heartbreaking.

The credit for the discovery of Pluto instead goes to Clyde Tombaugh, another Mars Hill staff member who spotted an intangible planet during a search in 1930 with his makeshift telescope built from old Buick parts. This ghostly planet would later be termed "Pluto," or god of the underworld, which was proposed by an eleven-year-old girl named Venetia Burney.

I love the wonder of all this: minds bending and slipping into the space where few can enter, where language can send us but also limit us at the same time. Sometimes, there aren't any words to give a shape or name to what we find.

· • ·

After my sister died in a car accident, I immersed myself in language, like I did when I was a kid. I buried myself in unfamiliar books about DNA, evolution, physics, astronomy, things I didn't understand. I wanted to find answers or, at the very least, patterns, so I'd know what to look for and how to prevent another loss. The more I obsessed, the more blurred the answers became. Even words couldn't provide the same comfort and security they had when I was a child.

The English word "conscious" was derived from the Latin "conscius" (con, "together" + scire, "to know.") But "conscius" meant "knowing with or having shared knowledge with another." In its earliest usages in the 1500s, the English word "conscious" held the Latin meaning. Thomas Hobbes in *Leviathan* wrote: "Where two, or more men, know one and the same fact, they are said to be Conscious of it one to another."

Which makes me think of the subconscious. Of everything under/below/beneath/besides. There's so much that's unpredictable.

Can we unlearn what we know? I've always loved William James: consciousness is a stream. Or wave. A continuous fluctuation of images throughout the mind. It rests, takes flight, roams, drifts. I think of foggy pregnancy days: senses were heightened (I could smell bad breath a foot away), but memory faded. Even more so the second time around. Once my daughter asked me what a half man, half horse was called. I saw the image in my head: a muscled man torso placed on top of a horse's defined body. The word slipped from memory.

I was restless, agitated. It drove me mad. I paced for several minutes, kicking things, trying to remember the damn word, but the closer I got the more pathetic my variations became. *Centile. Caesura. Censor. Damn.* Finally, when I was sitting on the porch, staring into the yard, not at all obsessing over it, the word emerged: *Centaur! Centaur!*

.   .   .

In 2005, the *trans-Neptunian* object "Eris" emerged. By *trans-Neptunian* they mean any object in the solar system that orbits the sun at a greater distance than Neptune. Eris complicated already-complex things. *Trans* = Latin noun or prefix: "across," "beyond," or "on the opposite side." It was so slight, near infinitesimal, considering that it was smaller than the smallest planet, Pluto. They couldn't have another small one. That was Pluto's role. Besides, it complicated things. So the International Astronomical Union redefined a planet as "a body that orbits the sun, is massive enough for its own gravity to make it round, and also has cleared its neighborhood of smaller objects around its orbit." Under this new definition, Pluto and other trans-Neptunian objects fell short and were demoted.

During my research, I stumbled upon the Kuiper Belt on the NASA website. It's an amazing cluster of objects orbiting in a disc-like zone outside the scope of Neptune. Pluto is a member of this far-flung other world multiplying with thousands of tiny ice worlds. These miniature worlds formed early in the history of our solar system. They offer some of the best evidence of the origins of our solar system. Or of us. Imagine our histories folding in, folding out. This is language.

I realized within my obsessive pursuit that the demotion or the renaming of Pluto represented another loss in my history, in my making. It's a reminder of how little control we have in this universe. It's unsettling. Eight planets just doesn't feel right or accurate. Despite its renaming, I'm also strangely attracted to it all the more: the way it embodies that uncomfortable yet alluring space between question and answer, science and wonder, intellect and materiality. The distance between these dualities isn't quite as defined as language has made it out to be. This means there is so much more to explore, even if there are no sound answers.

TEN YEARS AFTER

I'm sitting in my car sipping hot chocolate. I'm listening to Pearl Jam. You loved Pearl Jam. At least I think you did. I know I always did. Somehow your past is my past. Or my past is your past.

It's been ten years since you died. This is supposed to be important. A milestone in grief? You died in 2001. Three months to the day after September 11th. This is how I count the years. *Eleven + Eleven = Twenty-two*. Which was your favorite number. My birthday is September 22nd. You resented me for this.

It's dark outside. Headstones are silver at night. Like rain. It's close to Christmas, so the cemetery is lit up with battery operated Christmas trees. They flicker red and green and blue. I light a candle. The wind blows out the flame, so I have it in the car. It smells like cinnamon.

I don't know what I'm looking for today. I don't know what the numbers mean.

I smoke a cigarette. I don't smoke, but I keep a pack in my car for emergency situations. Tonight is one. I'm cold. My fingers feel like they might break off. The smoke burns my eyes. I never liked the smell. I'm nervous. I'm restless. I need something to occupy my energy. It's a wonder I never became addicted. I can hear you: "Stop fidgeting, Liz. Sit still."

You told Dad once just for the hell of it that I was a smoker. I was fourteen. I got in trouble, was lectured, had to stay in for two nights. I begged you to tell him that it wasn't true. You thought it was funny. I don't know if you ever did tell him it wasn't true. Maybe he still thinks I do. I don't know.

You always pulled these stunts, were always in trouble. The one who crashed Dad's truck twice, who got caught the most. I always felt like I had a protective layer of skin with you around. After you died I felt exposed, like I was walking around with all my nerve endings inside out.

I'm waiting for something. I don't know what. I watched family members speak in memory of their loved ones on September 11, 2011, ten years after, on the news. A woman who lost her niece said the day marked a new beginning, an ending to the mourning that had shadowed and surrounded them for ten years. It meant a time for celebration for the time spent.

I can't celebrate. I'm sorry. I'm here drinking hot chocolate with you. I have candy canes. You loved peppermint.

It's close to 8 pm. I came here alone. I told Bret to stay behind. He wanted to be here too. Remember how you once said you couldn't imagine me dating anyone else because you loved Bret so much? We got married on the edge of a cliff overlooking the Pacific Ocean five years ago. I wish you could have been there. It was beautiful and terrifying. Love is like that. I also came with Mom earlier. I can't begin to understand the magnitude of her pain.

I wanted to separate my grief from theirs. I'm playing the music louder. Now I'm listening to Counting Crows because I'm positive you loved Counting Crows. I remember sitting in Dad's car with you, blaring this song as we swerved through country roads.

Why did you have to die in December? It's already depressing this time of year. People are sad. Drunk. The trees are bare. They look like knobbed fingers.

I can't take it, so I get back out of my car and walk toward your grave. I'm lost. In daylight, I use the pine tree with a garbage bin attached by a chain to find your grave. If I walk in a straight line, twelve steps forward, I see you. In the darkness, the trees are all the same. I'm pretty sure someone has moved the bin.

I walk to the back. To the edge of the graveyard. I look for the bench that says, "In a blink of an eye, we'll be together again." It has sunflowers on it. This isn't your bench. It's a little girl's bench. She died in 1994. She was nine. It's close to your grave. I stumbled upon the girl's bench one day while wandering through the cemetery aimlessly, and stopped to read the inscription because I know you loved sunflowers. As ridiculous as it sounds, I can't help but think I stumbled upon that stone for a reason. The bench is cold and silver too. It's wet so I don't sit on it. I'm shivering now. I rub my hands together. I'm certain my lips are blue. I can hear you now: "Your lips are blue, Liz." I know.

It makes sense that you would be the one to die first. You were the one who took every chance before any of us, tried everything first, had all the kids first. Sometimes, I'm angry because of this. For once, couldn't you let me do something before you?

I find you in the moonlight. Your grave is wet and flat. Mom brought out a Christmas tree. My daughter brought you a candy cane earlier. I put another one down. This one is blue. It seems silly. I know. I never know what to do here. I try not to think about your bones, but I do. I try not to think about your hair, but I do.

I wish it snowed here. We grew up in snow. You should be buried in snow. The way we used to bury each other when we were little. Remember when you broke my wrist that winter by giving me a rocket? This was my second time breaking my wrist in three months, so I hated you for it. You felt horrible, bought me a stuffed reindeer with bells. And remember how I had to wrap a bag around the cast so I could play in the snow? I wasn't supposed to. I did anyway. I'm talking to myself now. Cemeteries will do that to you at night.

It's been so long since I've heard your voice. I think I remember the way it sounds. Then again, that's the way I make it sound. The farther away you go, the more I re-invent you, your time, our time, your past, our past. If I close my eyes, I think I hear it somewhere. Like rolling down the windows at night in the rain. If I listen closely, I can hear it drip into a can somewhere.

I think of rain dripping onto your casket. *Your casket. Your bones. Your hair. Casket. Bones. Hair. Fuck.* Now I'm crying and telling myself not to think of your casket, bones, hair. It's too much. You would laugh at me. You would tell me how I was over thinking everything again. You would tell me I was being emotional. I am. I am. I'm not. I'm not.

It didn't rain the day you died. It should have. It seems appropriate. Rain is silver and beautiful.

I should leave now. The battery operated Christmas trees are making me sad. Also, I'm getting scared. I'm sure strange people wander the cemetery at night. What kind of person goes to the cemetery at night, anyway?

I say goodbye to you again. Your bones. Your hair. I tell you I love you. I should be drinking a beer anyway. Why didn't I bring one? I tell you I'll drink a beer at home. But I won't celebrate. Beer makes me sad.

I walk away from you, back into my car where it's warm. I turn the radio back on. You would be thirty-five now. You were twenty-five when you died. I've passed you in age, which is odd because you're my older sister. Your two kids seem to have adjusted to life's circumstances, curves. Your oldest looks just like you at that age. Your youngest is lanky like you. He has your long, dainty fingers. It kills me I'm living and you aren't, that I get to see them grow and you don't. Even ten years later.

I have two now myself that you never met. I told you once that you would have all the kids for me. Amaya never met you but she talks about you. A few years ago, at her preschool, her teacher told me Amaya told her that her doll's name was Sarah. She never told me she named her that. She also told her she had a sister who died, whose name was Sarah, and it was very sad. Her teacher told me this was her way of trying to make sense of my loss.

I'm driving through the dark arc of the cemetery now. It's amazing how if you drive straight from each point of entry in the cemetery all the roads curve into one, and you end up back at the same place. That's the way I feel. That no matter which direction I go, what happens in my life, it always comes back to you.

I'm driving faster now. I want to see my kids. Bret. I want to drink a few beers. I want. I want. To sleep. To wake up tomorrow.

IT BEGINS

WITH ROUTINE

I arrived at Sarah's house around 6:30 am. I'm retracing these details from a distance. At this point in time, it's been almost nine years. It was a Tuesday, and I was there to watch her kids while she went to school because this is what I did. I babysat my nephews while she learned to be a nurse. I was twenty-three then. I remember her face as she opened the door that day, half shadowed, mascara smudged under eyes, her hair pulled into a messy bun. I don't remember what shirt she was wearing. Every time I try, I find myself inserting different shirts I knew she wore to bed frequently, but I'm not certain which one she had on that morning. This irritates me. I remember she told me she didn't need me to come over that day because she didn't have class. She said she called me the night before. I didn't remember the phone call, but I told her I would stay anyway. After all, I was already awake and there. I'm trying not to sentimentalize or romanticize things, but there is something magical about early mornings. The day hasn't quite unfolded and the house is quiet, heavy with sleep. When I revisit this early morning, it feels as if I'm sleepwalking. I remember drinking coffee with her while browsing Target's website. She was showing me gifts she bought the kids for Christmas. I remember my three-year-old nephew waking in a frantic frenzy, running to her arms, wanting to be held, not wanting to see me because he thought that meant his mom was leaving. When it was time to dress him for preschool, he wouldn't let me help. Instead, I fed her newborn a bottle. I offered to take my nephew to school, so she didn't have to get the baby dressed. She wanted to take him because normally she wouldn't get to do this. I didn't try to change her mind. I like to think I didn't because I was selfless, but in actuality I was exhausted. I was out late the night before and wanted to fall asleep with the baby.

She returned shortly after. Maybe it had been fifteen, twenty minutes. We watched Regis, while balancing the baby, rocking the baby, cooing and ohhhing at the baby. We marveled at his small body, small nose, ears, eyes, talked about his features, her features, his dad's features, his temperament versus her other son's temperament. Then something that always strikes me as odd. She brought up our dead grandfather, said she dreamed of him the night before, said it was creepy, but didn't give me any more details. I didn't press. Why would I?

WITH TRAGEDY

Recently I read the headline: INFANT DEAD AFTER MOTHER PUTS IN MICROWAVE. I couldn't read the story. I didn't want to know. There are some stories you don't want to step inside. I tried to stop there, but my imagination ran wild. I saw her pacing in the kitchen, the baby screaming, shrieking. She was frantic, shaking his small body, yanking his arms. She couldn't think straight, didn't think he was real. She tossed him on the couch, but his screams grew louder, piercing. She smoked a cigarette, hoping for silence, but its mouth was open, bursting, red and wide. She didn't want it, didn't want to see its eyes. She opened the microwave door—

WITH A SURPRISE

I remember thinking I could only have one child after I had my daughter because she was an accident. She caught me off guard, altered my world, rocked it, brought glints of laughter and love during grief. But with this overwhelming love came overwhelming anxiety. At night, I woke with sudden spasms in muscles. I was terrified of everything. So when Bret wanted another, I was afraid. I questioned this. I adjusted to chaos already, and our home functioned fine with just the three of us.

WITH A SUDDEN BLOW

This is the part of the Tuesday I obsess over the most. When it was time to pick my nephew up from preschool, we thought we would all go together. But then things got complicated. The baby was fussy, it was cold outside, and she didn't want to be late. I said I would go. Or did I? She was the one to leave. She returned once to grab a snack from the pantry for her son. I don't even know if I said anything. I know I was sitting on the couch, newborn in hand. I had class later that day. She knew this, so when she was late to return, at first I was angry. I planned on letting her know how upset I was when she returned. As more time went by, I panicked. This wasn't like her. There must have been something wrong. Shortly after, the doorbell rang, and I opened the door to two police officers, one of them a woman. The man asked if this was my sister's house. Yes. I kept searching the woman, who was intense, frowning. He asked if he could come inside to talk with me. After he entered, he glanced toward a picture on her credenza and asked if that was her, my sister. He shook his head. I started to panic. He told me to have a seat. In my mind, he spoke slowly, heavily. He said someone ran a stop sign and hit my sister's truck, causing it to flip, land upside down, strike a telephone pole. I couldn't comprehend his words. I heard what he said, but it didn't register. I didn't want to believe it. I asked him where she was. He said he was sorry, it was a fatality. I kept saying, She just left this house. She just left. He said he was sorry. My body shut down. I couldn't move or speak. I glanced toward her sleeping newborn. I wondered what he would do without her. And her older one at preschool, the one waiting for her to pick him up. Oh my god, I said. What about Bailey? He wasn't in the car? The chaplain told me at first they thought there were kids in the car because of the car seats, but they had searched the fields and found nothing. I told him he was still at preschool then, we needed to pick him up immediately. I yelled out the names of all the people we had to contact right away and grabbed the phone, but he guided me toward the table, told me to make a list. He said he would drive me to the preschool and to my mom's work. I called Bret and told him the news like this: My sister died in a car accident. I need you to come over right away. He stuttered, What? Where? What happened? Oh my god. What? I told him to get there as fast as possible. I couldn't find the language to explain something I also didn't understand to someone else.

WITH WANT

After a while, my body gave and craved another. After all, I couldn't function without chaos.

Anthropologist Meredith Smalls points out: "We also have all the pieces for the answer to why our infants are born so helpless. They are born with unfinished brains because the pelvis simply cannot be any wider or any bigger. If it were, women couldn't walk."

We've sacrificed finished brains for half finished brains in order to walk on two legs. Which means the nervous system is half developed.

WITH VULNERABILITY

Both of my babies, like all babies I'm sure, entered the world bloody and furious. Those initial seconds after the baby bursts into your arms are outside reality; there isn't much time to react. I remember seeing Bret hold Anderson in those blurry seconds, how his small, slippery head fit into his open palm, his body curved into the space between Bret's elbow and wrist. I thought it was beautiful and terrifying at once, how vulnerable we all are.

WITH NUMBNESS

My head felt heavy. I didn't know what hit me. I wanted to keep moving. Bret arrived quickly, bewildered, and pulled me close, crying. I kept looking at her sleeping newborn. I paced. Checked and rechecked the baby's blankets, making sure his face wasn't covered. I told Bret to keep the cat away from him. Sarah didn't want the cat near him. I told everyone I was fine to drive. I really didn't want to be trapped in the car with the chaplain, the man who told me my sister's accident was a fatality. Even he couldn't say the words, She's dead. So he talked around it, and we all moved around it. But this man embraced me under his arm, whispered he would drive me so I could process things. I didn't have the energy to argue so we loaded into my white Saturn. During the drive, I stared at the white sky and thought about strange things, like my political science final scheduled later that day, thank god I didn't have to take it, about her clothes at the cleaners. I told myself to pick them up later. I gave the chaplain directions, but he said he knew where to go. He took the freeway, bypassing the street where her accident was. I asked him to drive by the scene. I don't know why I wanted to go there. For some reason, I thought I could help or I needed to be there or maybe they were all wrong. He said it wasn't a good idea. I wondered who this man thought he was, exerting so much control over this tragedy. I resented him because I knew he was there and he saw her. My mind drifted off to her fiancé. How he didn't know yet because she had his cell phone. I told the chaplain we had to find a way to get a hold of him. He said not to worry, he would. When we pulled into the parking lot, I saw all of my nephew's teachers lined up. I didn't want to see them, didn't want to talk to them. When I got out, the director grabbed me, hugged me, told me over and over how sorry she was, that I was okay, to be strong. In that moment, I hated her. All of them. I wasn't ready. I turned away from the rest of the line of people extending arms toward me. It wasn't until I saw my nephew, gallantly running toward me, asking if I had candy for him, that I cried.

I remembered right then my sister came back once before leaving to grab a treat for him. She said she couldn't forget his surprise. I remember how surprised she was when she found out she was pregnant with him. How surprised we all were. How young she was. How she always said he turned her life around for the better. How she loved being a mom. Was made to be a mom. It was fruit snacks, I noted in my head. The chaplain took over, diverted my nephew's attention toward an airplane in the sky, asked him if he knew how to make paper airplanes, told him we were all going to his grandma's work. My nephew didn't question my strange behavior, the man in blue driving my car. He was just excited to see Grandma.

WITH URGENCY

I heard the chair collapse first, a splintering sound. I saw Bret's body unravel, infant in hand dangling, the bottle in the other. I couldn't stop it. I watched my baby fall to the floor, heard a low thud as his head struck hardwood, Bret's body sprawled out beside him, the shattered chair. Anderson shrieked. This cry was different. It had urgency, panic. But instead of going to him, to them, I ran into the other room. I hid from what I didn't want to see.

WITH DISCONNECTION

Not long ago, Dad called and told me the twelve-year-old who lived in our old house had died. He was struck by a car while riding his bike. I didn't know the boy. I only met him once. Dad lives behind our old house with his new family. One summer while I was visiting, the boy burst through his front door and asked if my step-sister was home. I said no. He asked if all the kids in the room were mine. I told him one was, the others were my nephews. He said he thought I looked too young to have so many kids. I remember thinking I thought he was smart, strange, frantic.

Now whenever I return to my hometown to visit Dad, I can't help but drive past our old house and think of us as kids running up and down the three flights of stairs. I also think of the twelve-year-old boy now, jogging up and down those same stairs, jumping into his bed that was inside the same bedroom I shared with my sisters, and I'm sad for all of us.

WITH HELPLESSNESS

I don't know how someone could ever tell a mother her child is dead. When we arrived at Mom's work, I thought I should tell her but froze, became speechless, and everything whirled past me quickly. My nephew ran into her arms as she kissed him, asking him if he wanted peppermints. She looked up toward the chaplain, confused, then at me, then at him, me again, and asked where my sister was. I knew she knew but didn't want to know. The chaplain leaned in close to her, bent down, put his arm around her, told her the news. She screamed before he could finish, stood up and ran past me, out the door, onto pavement, collapsing, crying. I wanted to help her but couldn't.

WITH FAILURE

The car ride to the hospital was a blur. Bret couldn't speak. He was distraught, worried, and kept saying he would never forgive himself if Anderson wasn't okay. I told him not to go there yet, I couldn't think that way. My stomach was in knots. Amaya kept saying on the ride over, This is so awful, Mommy. We pulled into the front of the hospital, and I got out with Anderson, bundled in my arms, while Bret parked the car with Amaya. The woman behind the barred counter sensed my urgency, desperation, told me to calm down, asked me what happened. I told her in jumbled phrases: He was dropped. I mean, he fell. It was the chair, his dad, it broke. It was an accident. She was gentle, kind, looked toward Anderson, told us to go to triage. When a nurse removed his clothes, he became hysterical. A young, female doctor emerged, shined a small light in his eyes. She waved her hand in front of him, then investigated his small body. She asked me a surge of questions. What happened? Did he land headfirst? Did he cry? Did he vomit? Is this the first time something like this has happened? He had only been here for ten days and I felt incompetent, like I was not fit to protect anyone from the heartbreaks of this world. I was bound to fail. I remember her saying, Screams are good, Mom. It's the silence that's concerning.

WITH UNCERTAINTY

No one wanted to tell my three-year-old nephew his mom was dead, she wasn't coming home. We postponed it, dreaded it, waited until the end of the day when we could no longer conceal it. We thought we should do it as a family, with my mom, sister, brother, uncle and my sister's fiancé all in tow. I don't remember who said the words, but I know he hopped in my lap and looked at me for some security and how at that very moment I believed there was no such thing. The two of us became connected by uncertainty.

WITH AN ENDING

When the doctor told Bret and me our baby was fine, I couldn't believe it. They didn't want to run a CAT scan because there were no visible signs of damage, no bruises or bumps. The baby was responsive, agitated. All of which was good, the doctor kept saying. I imagined there was something hidden, like a bruise on the brain no one could see, located in some gray area. It was bleeding, but no one would know until something snapped, triggering something else no one saw coming. I asked how likely it was he suffered brain damage. She said it was slim. I only thought of the slim margins of error: the woman tossing her infant in a microwave, the twelve-year-old boy, what my father's face must have looked like when my uncle drove to his house to tell him the news, my mother's grief, my sister's fiancé's silence as he opened the door to find a house full of relatives and fruit salads, my brother on the other end of the phone, repeating, What, No, What, my sister pulling over on the side of I-5 as she struggled to make sense of Mom's words, crying, cars blowing past her on the freeway. Seconds before, they all thought they were unscathed.

JELLYFISH

These days, I imagine my neighbors as pedophiles peeking in windows, watching my three-year-old daughter, Amaya, play in the front lawn, watching her white knuckles bend and unbend as she pulls roots. They wait for the slight chance I'll leave her alone, go inside and wash the dishes or grab a jacket or tea, disappearing for a few seconds, so they can snatch her and launch their escape plan: slip through the neighbor's gate, hopping over the back fence, ending up on the street behind us where a car awaits, the motor humming, ready to sputter off, leaving a cloud of smoke. I see them standing in lawns, pretending to water gardens. I know their secrets: I hear their pencils sketching into notebooks late at night, devising plans, making blueprints. I won't let them take her.

I want to believe this is normal behavior. A friend confirms this: "Of course, now that you're a mother, everything is heightened." Sounds are heightened: I cover my ears as she writes her name in chalk on the sidewalk.

I think of the four-year-old girl on the news, snatched from the front of her house while writing with chalk on the sidewalk, the one with curly locks, a round face, the one who screamed, "Noooo!" Her mother said, "She did everything I taught her—kicked, screamed, bit skin, but nobody could reach her in time." Her grandmother washed dishes inside, glancing up occasionally through the window above the sink. The sound of water and clanking dishes drowned out her yells.

.   •   .

An aunt calls to tell me she had a dream about me. "You were shielding Amaya from a vulture that kept swooping in over her." She always does this—calls me with a weird dream, somehow eerily similar to something that's happening in my life.

I tell her that her dream confirms my fears: pedophiles are swarming our lawn, trying to swipe my daughter. I'm obsessing—closing blinds, shunning neighbors. "That's not normal behavior," she says. "Don't all mothers worry?" I ask. "Not to the point of paralysis. It sounds more like a defense mechanism."

.   •   .

"Have you scanned the area for pedophiles?" my mother asks when I explain my nightmares. I had. I noted several houses in the area, smeared with red dots. *Sexual assault against a minor. Lewd and lascivious behavior.* Their faces stuck in my head. Some looked like nice grandfathers, unsuspecting. Of course, Amaya is unsuspecting. She waves at the mailman, asks him if he wants to blow bubbles. I tell her no—don't trust anyone. I tell her the world is dangerous, filled with dangerous people who want to do dangerous things to unsuspecting children.

"That's going too far," Bret says. "You're going to raise her to be scared of the world."

.   •   .

A recurring dream: in a lake I see my reflection, a fish, bony flesh. It turns its eye toward me, piercing blue. I want to hold it, but it swims through my fingers, its scales sharp as the edges of feathers, flesh like wet hair.

.   •   .

At the Monterey Bay Aquarium, Amaya is obsessed with jellyfish. She loves their bodies, curved like bells. I tell her they act similar to the brain, malleable, flexible. She wants to hold their tentacles. "It's like hair," she says. She presses her hand against the glass. "They're staring at me." I'm also amazed at how they perceive their world using small organs that function as eyes attached to their threadlike tentacles. They can sense variations of light with a heightened sensitivity to red. Unable to communicate with each other because they lack a brain, they use senses in tentacles to detect danger and sting prey.

.   •   .

As it turns out, there's a fish inside all of us. Or in the words of paleontologist, Neil Shubin: "If we follow the gill arches from an embryo to an adult, we can trace the origins of jaws, ears, larynx, and throat. Bones, muscles, nerves, and arteries all develop inside these gill arches. Our skulls lose all evidence of their segmental origins as we go from embryo to adult. The plate like bones of our skulls form over gill arches."

In other words, follow the patterns: I'm teaching her to write the letters of the alphabet. Trace the lines and follow the patterns. I hold her hand in mine as we make the arch of a U. "It looks like a mouth," she says. "Or an upside down bell," I say. "Like the jellyfish," she says.

· • ·

In my mother's recurring dream, she chases after my dead sister in woods, but each time she gets closer my sister's face turns into my mother's dead brother. "But the weird thing is that I never met that brother," she says.

It's the truth. My mother once told me how her mother was expecting twins, but one died before reaching air, the other had smothered it on the way out. Imagine the dichotomy. One comes out red and alive, and the other comes out blue and dead. She can't get the texture out of her head. As she reached for my sister's hair, she pulled a piece that was coarse and salty as seaweed.

Sometimes, my mother stares hard into the distance, and her eyes become pearls as if she's left this place. I wonder if she's chasing a dead or live child as her body sways between lines of light.

. • .

What it comes down to is this: memories and stories are colliding inside brains, shaping us, reinventing our scripts. I believe I have died many small deaths. There's an animal inside all of us, and the instinct that drives us toward death is the same instinct that drives us toward life. Our desires change. Our brains are malleable. This is how we survive, how we protect and adapt. I'm choosing to be afraid to protect what's mine because there's nothing so as ambiguous as time. What's in front of me is vanishing.

LOCKDOWN

It's Wednesday, 1:01 pm, and I'm pulling in to pick up Amaya from kindergarten. A helicopter circles overhead. A voice from a white afternoon sky yells, "Come out immediately or you will be bit by dogs." And dogs, K-9s, are pulling blue uniformed police officers throughout the school. I've just arrived and I'm trying to take this all in: blinking lights, barking, walkie-talkies. I barely pull to a stop before unlatching my seatbelt, my car hanging off the curb. A voice next to me says, "Ma'am, ma'am, you can't. . . . " but I have tunnel vision. Also known as Kalnienk Vision. All I can see is the silver gate ahead, her classroom door, Room 4, tightly sealed. I'm going to climb the fence to get there. I race forward, my eyes locked on number 4, and I'm stopped, pulled to the side by another mom, who says, "They're on lockdown." LOCK. DOWN. The words vibrate through my skull, shuddering through sternum, down to knees, buckling. The other mom grips my arm, holding me up, "Don't panic." I repeat her words, "Lock down? Lockdown?" As in: no one comes out and no one comes in. A mother's imagination is a dangerous space:

fears tangle with nightmares and newspaper clippings and childhood scars and friends' of friends' stories of tragedies. This is what ignites us, propels us into full-blown panic, a hyper-aware, hypersensitive, hyper-driven state. It shuts off all other zones in brains, turning off all voices telling us we're fine, everything is okay, we're overreacting. Our body locks down. So when I hear the word *lockdown*, it triggers synapses and associations and I think of Columbine. Of caliber guns. Of closed windows. Heads under desks. Covering her ears. Arms enwrapping small bodies. Bullets. Of her biting her hair. Of the bruise on her knee. A woodchip in her shoe. Feet stomping on the roof above her. Her voice, singing, "Who ate the alphabet?" The woman next to me pulls me from this space and says, "I just heard they're after a burglar who robbed a house in the area, who was seen by a neighbor, who called the police, who arrived just before he fled. He's on parole." I think of what we're capable of doing if our safety or life is threatened. Of that dangerous space inside the mind that shuts and locks out others. Of tunnel vision. Of being trapped. Of only seeing one-way out. Of the principle's voice on the loudspeaker, "WE'RE STILL ON LOCKDOWN. DO NOT LEAVE THE CLASSROOM." Of the voice from the sky, "SURRENDER IMMEDIATELY OR YOU WILL BE BIT." Of a man on the run. Of small hostages. Of knives. Suicide. A gun to a head. The blow. The noise. Because in this space, no one escapes the blow: kids in khakis and polo tops don't race out doors to mothers who collapse on grass, sobbing, pulling their children to chests, a criminal doesn't slip through a hole in the fence into a neighboring backyard, teachers don't sigh with relief, sirens don't turn off, parents don't drive to

7-Elevens for cheer-up Slurpee's, dogs don't sit near curbs, resting. In this space, we forget what safety and comfort are, of what is and isn't reality and we linger there, locking up the narratives that tell us otherwise, some of us never making it out.

DOOR COLLECTING

I met a man who sells old chipped doors. He was standing outside on his lawn with all of them lined up like statues against his house. I had to stop. I wanted to turn each knob. To enter each door. He said he collected them. That no two were the same.

Bret hates that I collect so many old things. He likes new. Polished.

In 1925, snowflake-obsessed photographer Wilson A. Bentley wrote: "Under the microscope, I found that snowflakes were miracles of beauty, and it seemed a shame that this beauty should not be seen and appreciated by others. Every crystal was a masterpiece of design and no design was ever repeated."

To obsess is to think about something relentlessly. A thought becomes an obsession when it takes over all other thoughts. It haunts. Dwells. Dominates. Distracts us from unwanted emotions. There is a question as to what is conscious here—do we choose it or does it choose us? Do we allow it to control us or do we surrender ourselves to its control?

Each winter, my brother constructed intricate snow forts. He was known in the neighborhood as the best, but was exclusive in who was allowed in each hideout. After all, he spent many hours crafting each one. The fort I remember most was built on the edge of a hill, so you had to enter by tunnel. Inside everything was eerily quiet. Voices and small sounds seemed to echo like pins. Like slipping inside a cocoon. Everything was white. But also: specks of blue.

When I'm cold, my lips turn blue. This is called cyanosis, which means a bluish tint to the skin or mucus membranes. So during winters, I was self-conscious of the blue tint beneath my skin, my blue lips. I felt like a blue dot on a white sheet of paper. I have an abnormal valve. Or in more clinical terms, I was born with pulmonary valve stenosis, a valve disorder that entails the pulmonary valve, which divides the right ventricle (one of the main chambers in the heart) and the pulmonary artery. This artery carries oxygen-poor blood to lungs, and stenosis occurs when the valve can't open wide enough, which means less blood flow to the lungs. If you put your hand to my chest, you can feel it close in a quick shudder. Every time I go to the doctor for a routine check-up, and they take their stethoscope to my chest, they jump back. "Wow. That's quite a murmur you have there. Have you had your heart checked out before?"

After many winters, Mom began to hate the snow in Wisconsin. Some days it trapped us inside. Piling up outside our front door. She missed the sunlight and was bored with all that glaring white. Every now and then if you look closely, you can see flashes of blue streak through the white snow. Winters were long and blue for her. After work, Dad stopped off at local bars to wind down from long days at work, losing himself in warm beer, the language of strangers, the collective conversation of demands and pressures. I remember my mom sitting on the couch in front of our large picture window, staring, disappearing in all that snow.

I'm thinking of the snowball effect, a figurative term for a string of events that begins relatively small and keeps building upon one another, becoming larger, more serious, and even dangerous or disastrous. As in: a vicious circle. A spiral of decline. One thing triggers the next. And so on.

Like me, Mom also collects interesting objects from yard sales. I called her to meet the man who sells old doors. She met me there. She wanted a yellow one. He said to place it up against a white wall so the color would pop. Mom has an eye for arrangement. She sees the spaces in her head and measures it accordingly and everything fits perfectly. I never plan ahead. I collect the objects and place them as inconsistently as possible. To her, this is clutter. In my clutter I find consistency.

Dad collected coins. Each night, he emptied his pockets, placing each coin into his top drawer. Eventually it got so full, it was hard to open the drawer. Mom begged him to do something with them. To her, this was disorder. So he would give them to me to count and roll up in money rolls. Then he would take me to the bank, so I could cash them in. Before long, like magic, his drawer filled with coins again.

Anthropologist, Marjorie Akin writes in her essay, "Passionate Possession: The Formation of Private Collections": "Objects can connect the collector to the historic, valued past." She also says that another reason to collect is for the collector's need to be complete. Like we're in a continuous state of piecing our past together with objects.

This is why we clutch to photographs. As untruthful as they are. Many of the photos of my childhood have been lost in between all the moves. My childhood is like a flurry of images I've collected or seen at some point before they've disappeared. I've tried to reassemble a story.

Wallace Stevens: "A violent order is disorder; and a great disorder is an order. These two things are one."

When I was young, I collected rocks. We lived on a dead end. The edge of our block was a gravel circle cars turned around on. My sisters and I spent many hours collecting rocks we stored in brown paper bags. At night we dumped them out and compared treasures. Sometimes, we made trades. For me, collecting the rocks was more about the exploration. The hours spent, bending, mulling through gravel, finding a speck of blue in dust or a fossil among boulders. Sometimes, I used a hammer to break them open to see if crystals were inside. Collecting objects is like collecting facts.

Every year until I turned seventeen, I had to have an electrocardiogram, also known as an EKG. Doctors wanted to monitor my heart and check for fluctuations. Leakages. I mostly remember Dad taking me to these uncomfortable appointments. He waited outside the room, so I was alone with the cardiologists and their plastic hands. I was always terrified of these appointments because I thought the doctors were going to tell me I was dying, I didn't have very long to live, and if they didn't tell me, they knew it, and were going to keep it a secret from me. Inside these cold rooms, I would lie on a vinyl bed, awkwardly, in a paper gown, open in front, my heart exposed to all, their cold hands pressing sticky electrodes attached by wires to my chest and arms. I lost myself in the electricity. I listened to it whistle. Hum. Buzz. I watched doctors get animated at the sound of each inconsistency, each twist. They whispered to each other, "There it is. Do you hear that? Listen." I stared at the screen, watching lines curve and drop. They were obsessed with understanding its language. How quickly it could change tone. Speed. How different each heart beat could be. Like they were piecing together a pattern and they could predict what would happen next. Each time, every year, I disappeared in those curves.

Like me, I imagine the man who collects doors is trying to piece his way back somewhere.

Oddly enough, the preschool I briefly attended was called "Humpty Dumpty." My parents gave up after a few months because I wrapped my body around their legs and screamed when they tried to leave. Every day, we recited the lyrics: "Humpty Dumpty sat on a wall.

Humpty Dumpty had a great fall. All the king's horses and all the king's men couldn't put Humpty together again." In Lewis Carroll's *Through The Looking Glass*, Humpty Dumpty says, "It means just what I choose it to mean—neither more nor less." After which, Alice says, "The question is whether you can make words mean so many different things."

Or is it, what we thought we forgot resurfaces in our collections. Haunts us. All these objects representative of so many different diversions. Places. Like words. If we can piece them together, we might have a map.

In the language of snow: a dendrite is a complex hexagonal crystal with fern-like branches; a polycrystal is a snowflake consisting of multiple ice crystals; a snow flurry is snow that falls for short intervals, changing in intensity; a snow squall is a short but intense fall of snow that shrinks visibility; a snowburst is a very intense fall shower of snow, short in duration, hampering visibility; a watermelon snow is snow with red algae growing on it; a whiteout is a state in which daylight is dimmed by multiple reflections between a snow surface and an overcast sky, vanishing the horizon.

In 1924, Dutch physiologist, Willem Einthoven was granted the Nobel Prize in Physiology or Medicine for his invention of a string galvanometer, which he used to create an electrocardiogram, a physical recording of the electrical activity of the heart. Einthoven wanted to record the heartbeat as early as 1891. At that time, a tool called the capillary electrometer was used to record alterations of electrical potential caused by spasms of the heart muscle. It wasn't accurate and Einthoven wanted precision. In 1903, he designed a string galvanometer, a slim line of quartz held in a magnetic field. As electric current flowed through the wire, it moved. The wire's motion was magnified and projected onto a moving photographic film. This allowed accurate measurements of a heart's electrical action, and this machine revolutionized medicine. He named this the electrocardiograph. The chart created by the instrument is known as an EKG, an abbreviation for the German word *Elektrokardiogramm*. Einthoven explained how to situate the electrodes in his machine, clarified a pattern made by regular heart waves and showed how to translate electrocardiograms.

I'm insecure of my heart. Sometimes, I feel like I'm walking around inside out and my misshapen valve is visible to all. Often I place my hand across my chest to cover it, protect it. The buzz comforts me. I'm never comfortable with silence. At night, I sleep with my palm pressed to my heart.

Eventually, Mom moved us to California to see more sunlight. She wanted to be closer to her family, leave the blue winters behind. She wanted a remedy for her loneliness. Dad got a new job wearing suits. He was bored and miserable. He missed what he left behind. Every night, empty silver cans of beer collected on the counter.

Interestingly enough, Founding Father of the United States, Benjamin Rush has also been termed the "Father of American Psychiatry." In 1812, he published the first textbook on the subject in the United States, *Medical*

Inquiries and Observations upon the Diseases of the Mind.
He initiated a therapeutic approach to addiction. At
that time, alcoholism was termed "inebriety," and it was
seen as sinful and the result of bad choices. However,
Rush believed the alcoholic lost control over himself,
letting the addiction or disease take control.

Bentley was obsessed with the snowflake. He was relentless. Through years of trial and error, in 1885, he became the first to capture a single snow crystal in a pho-
tograph. In his lifetime, he captured more than 5,000
snowflakes. Like he said, no two were alike.

Current EKG machines are still based on Einthoven's
original invention. The device illustrates a series of
waves related to electrical impulses that happen during each heartbeat. In a normal record, the waves are
termed P, Q, R, S, and T and follow in alphabetical
order. When the waves follow the order defined al-
phabetically, the heart is said to show a normal sinus
rhythm and pulses may be understood as following the
regular conduction path. The heart is depicted as dis-
playing arrhythmia or dysrhythmia when time intervals between waves, the order, or the number of waves
doesn't fit within this pattern.

Most of the doors the man collects are broken. They
don't quite shut all the way, or there's a missing hinge,
or the glass knob is missing or chipped. I'm attracted to
such beautiful misshapen idiosyncrasies.

When I was four, my grandpa had a heart attack while
we were visiting him. To distract me from what was

happening, my parents gave me a pile of coins to play with. I remember piling them on top of one another, building a tower. I wanted them to shine, so I placed each one onto my tongue. When the paramedics and fire squad entered through the front door, I swallowed hard, choking and gasping. I thought they were coming for me.

I never knew Mom was an alcoholic because she drank alone. Each night she tucked me into bed—reading me books, reciting prayers, blessing me, pulling the covers tight to my chest—then she closed the door. She insists alcoholism took control of her, defined her and kept her distracted from unwanted emotions. She says drinking became part of her routine and, once she started, she couldn't stop. She says she felt like she needed it to survive. In my mind it was the opposite. She always was present.

We collect and obsess to distract us from the present.

In 1611, German astronomer, mathematician, and astrologer Johannes Kepler published a short article, titled, *On the Six-Cornered Snowflake.* In this wandering meditation, he describes a snowflake as the perfect "Christmas present, since it comes down from heaven and looks like a star." He wondered why single snowflakes fell with six corners and speculated it was possibly because of the hexagon, which was one of only three shapes along with the triangle and square that fill up a plane without leaving spaces. He couldn't make sense of it and ruminated the question in a shape-shifting essay.

This is about the space inside a question. A puzzle. To wander. To speculate.

After we moved to California, my parents divorced and Dad moved back to Wisconsin with my sisters. Mom quit drinking. My sisters moved back and forth often between states, parents. After the divorce, it seemed Mom never felt settled and we moved all the time so she could re-decorate and reinvent her space with new furniture and objects. I loved watching the way she moved from room to room in a flurry. House to house. Apartment to apartment. Like a gypsy. It seemed her body never touched anything. If she stopped, the past would catch up with her.

Recently, her past resurfaced in a dream of my father and snow. When she reached to hold the snow, it didn't slip through her hands like powder. It was heavy and sharp like a crystal. A star. It shimmered in various colors like a kaleidoscope. Dad handed her a crystal tree branch, and she asked him what it was for. He said, "The shape reminds me of you." She called me the next day to tell me about it. "Isn't that strange, she said. " I haven't thought of him in so long."

It took me a while to trust Bret's hand across my heart. Finally, I let him press his hand over my heart at night. It was strange at first. I wanted to fight it. To control his hand. But eventually, it felt natural, and there was an unsettling and appealing attraction that came with be-ing in his palm.

Is the obsession in the incompletion or within the state of completion? Or is there ever a state of completion?

Isn't this why we love snow? How it disappears and comes back again. Snow scientists still marvel in its shape-shifting nature. They can't predict an onset of snowstorms and their consequences very far in advance. The unknown is unsettling and enthralling.

Mom bought the yellow door and left it in her garage. After trying it out in various places throughout her house, she decided that it didn't fit. So she placed it up against a stark wall. She has the cleanest and most orderly garage I've ever seen. There's not much in there, besides her white Explorer and garbage bins and a broom and litter box. Now there's a yellow door that pops. It grabs your attention. If you open the door and step through the frame, you'll hit a wall.

I'm obsessed with pursuit. The association. I'm relentless in my obsession with collecting. For a sense of completion. To come to terms with my past. To bring my sister back. There's no completion in grief. No matter how many doors I slip through, what's on the other side is always the same.

SO MUCH DEPENDS UPON
A CREDENZA

It's the year everything falls apart.

My 15-month-old son pulls the drawer off the old credenza. We don't fix it. We leave it broken. I like looking at the stuff I've crammed inside. Coins. Papers. Rocks. Melted candles. Keys. Books. Photos.

Mom says it's a conversation piece.

Bret says I'm a pack rat.

Because it's so old, I love it. Because it's so old, he hates it.

This is the year I'll hate to fly. The sound of the wheels unfolding scares me. The unexpected drops.

At Albany International Airport, I read about the Clocktower Project. I pause to lose myself in the language. Synaesthetic. Heart. Symbiotic. Bells. Time. Phosphorescent. Ring. Transformation. Light.

Metallic. Algorithmic. I feel as though I've been propelled inward.

One day, while on my way home from coffee with my sister, I see the credenza perched at the edge of a curb with a toilet beside it and a man waving his arms. Heather says, "Look at that man standing in the rain."

I think it's the most beautiful and sad thing that I've ever seen. I'm infatuated with the juxtaposition of beautiful and sad.

I pull to a stop and get out to run my fingers on it. I already know I want it, but I need to feel the texture. It's soggy. Worn. Smooth. Sharp edges. How much?

This is the year scientists report: light creates the complicated force called lift. Airfoils generate lift. As in: an engine propels a plane forward, its cambered wings cause it to rise.

This is the year the world is obsessed with the apocalypse.

In 1996, Christina Kubisch, a classically trained musician and professor of experimental art, visited the Massachusetts Museum of Contemporary Art. She was struck by the century-old factory clock—it hadn't kept time, its bells hadn't rung since 1986 when the Sprague Electric Co. vacated this 13-acre site.

The man says, "For you $40 and I'll throw in the toilet."

I tell him that I don't need the toilet, but I really want the credenza, although I don't have room for it in my car.

"I'll throw it in the back of my pick-up and follow you to your house," he says.

On the drive there, Heather asks where I'll put it.

I had already envisioned it by my front door with my green porcelain vase atop.

Since 1895, this 19th century clock had set the cadence of the workday, drumming every quarter hour.

Light foils won't keep an Airbus aloft for very long.

This is the year I feel lost in a fleeting world. I'm still running from the real source of pain that I'm afraid of losing everything around me. I feel transient in my own house and skin.

At my house, the man backs his red Toyota into my driveway and unloads the sad credenza. I give him $40. I stare at it for a while. Heather tells me to buy new knobs and paint it.

There's something incredibly attractive about a decrepit piece of furniture. It holds so much history, so many stories.

I move the three-year-old credenza Bret bought into my office and move the old one in its place. I open the cabinets and breathe in the smell. Old hands. Wet paper. I think of the layers of lives that have been taken in and out. So many beautiful stories weaved through time.

I'm reminded of my great-grandmother's buffet. It was given to my mom after she died. I remember the refinished wood. Brass knobs. All the photos stored inside. My small body used to fit in between the two shelves. I hid there many times during games of Hide 'n' Seek with my siblings. It was dark and smelled like fresh pine. Not a speck of dirt.

When Bret gets home from work, he says, "That's the ugliest thing I've ever seen."

Why is there such a gap between old and new. Beautiful and ugly.

Why is each end so definitive.

Because I love it, his words hit me like stars, in multiple ways, at my very core.

This is how we navigate life, angled.

Now researchers have created tiny rods shaped like airplane wings. They found when these micron-sized light foils were absorbed in water and hit with 130 milliwatts of light from the bottom of the chamber, they started to move up, as expected. But the rods also began moving to the side, a direction perpendicular to the incoming light.

Kubisch played the bells as though they were musical instruments. Ringing them with clappers. Beating.

Brushing. Striking them with her hands and other tools. She then recorded the bell tone database with a digital audio recorder.

This is the year Amaya turns four. She's simultaneously the happiest and saddest person I know. Some minutes her markers make her sad. The red isn't bright enough. There isn't enough pink. Or she has too many yellows and today she hates yellow. She needs orange. Other minutes, she picks me wildflowers from the backyard, placing them in cups of water. "Aren't they beautiful, Mommy?" In these moments, she runs through overgrown grass, laughing and even the wind slants toward her sound.

I'm trying to figure out what makes something stay afloat.

I'm afraid to sleep. I feel too trapped in my small frame. Even my bones hurt. I count the images.
We all want answers—some sense of order—as imagined as it may be.

Riding a beam of light, a tiny particle thousandths of millimeters in size is pushed sideways by the same force that keeps airplanes aloft.

Kubisch placed small solar senses in a band that surrounded the tower. Which relays the power of the sun to a computer inside the tower. Which is then translated by a software program, which provides her prerecorded bell sounds in response to light conditions.

We begin to refinish the kitchen, but stop midway through. We talk about painting the cabinets gray. Mosaic tile. We buy shiny black appliances. "Easier to clean," says the salesman. Bret installs a white Corian counter. It doesn't scratch. Hot pans won't leave a mark. A double sink. A new flexible faucet, easy to maneuver. We pull out the old backdrop. He redoes the drywall. We find newspapers dated as far back as 1957 inside. Small wasted women in high skirts pose in advertisements. Big smiles. Everyone is happy between walls. He builds a wine rack. We fill it with red wine. We grow weary. Bret is worried about numbers—will he get back what he put in? We never paint the cabinets. Or paint the wine rack. Or install the mosaic tile.

We bought this house with my nephews in mind. At the time, I was watching the youngest three days a week, and the older one, who lived with his father in New York, now visited in the summers. We wanted a yard for them to run around in.

What is it about unfinished projects. Is it the duration between. Those moments spent thinking about completion. The buildup. The temporary suspension.

I suppose that's the thrill in bungee jumping. The downward plunge. The moment your body is temporarily suspended in air, dangling. At eighteen, I fell backwards off a 50-foot platform. I felt my lungs close as I opened my mouth to scream, but nothing came out. I remember the terror of coming close, inches between my body and the earth.

Is that why jumping is the most popular form of suicide? Perhaps the end seems too far from sight. Too hard to visualize. Instead the gaze is fixed upon the space between. The blue sky.

Our neighbors short sell their house for $150,000. We bought ours for $264,000.

Because numbers sound so permanent. Un-wavering.

It's true we're always let down after the grand finale. Consider the light show on Christmas Tree Lane. Every year, we glide down the lane with our windows down, staring at strings of lights strung from trees. Each house gets brighter as we move forward. Amaya wants us to drive faster, to get closer toward the end. She knows at the end of the block, there are four houses outshining the rest. Once there, we're blinded by chaos. LED lights. They blink in accordance with blasting music. Tran-Siberian Orchestra. Statues of Rudolf, Santa and Jesus Christ flash and wave simultaneously. She's disappointed with the ending. We want more.

Boards slide off the fence between our house and the neighbor's. Our dog runs in and out.

This is the year that while walking Christmas Tree Lane, we witness a small dog run over. The driver is confused by the fog. The massive number of people. The chaos. He never sees the dog. He only feels the thud under his tire as he runs it over. I cover Amaya's eyes as the owner runs to pick up her bloodied dog, panting. She repeatedly asks: "Are the dog's eyes open?"

At what point does closure become an opening.

I realize again I'm trying to hold my house together because I'm trying to hold myself together. For some illogical reason, I've convinced myself I'm doing this for my sister, I'll disappoint her if I lose, or if I keep moving forward so quickly, I'll forget her.

I'm living like a transient, clenching onto the past and future, while swiftly twisting through the present.

It's a gray winter afternoon in North Adams, Massachusetts. In accordance with the weather, hushed sounds from the clocktower whisper the air.

Eventually, he piles bricks over the open slabs of wood in the fence.

I buy new knobs for the credenza but like the knobs better unattached. I like the credenza unfinished. I'm still running from endings.

Oranges don't bloom from our trees this year. Or lemons.

This is the year I also see the thin spine of a homeless woman. It's 105 degrees in Fresno. Her half naked body slides into the green canal water for a swim.

At what point does an ending become a beginning.

On hot summer days, the clock tower generates loud and metallic ringing into the sky.

Weather is unpredictable.

He says he can't stay in this house any longer. It's old. It's falling apart. We paid too much for it and we'll never get our money back. We should just leave. I realize, for me, this means also leaving my sister behind in a way that makes no sound sense, especially because she had never even been to this house. Whenever I encounter any kind of loss, her loss absorbs it. I re-experience it and go into shock.

At night, the clock tower project falls silent.

So the world must sleep.

This is the year they report the housing collapse left 10.7 million families owing more than their homes are worth.

Also that an increased number of young people are walking away from religious organizations.

Such is the language of collapse. Downward. Decline. Decrepit. Despair. Disappear.

Under the weather. Underpaid. Underwater.

During grief, your body feels like it's underwater sometimes, and you're submerged under life. Sometimes you emerge, but some days you're sucked back under with no explanation. You have no sense of time. It moves over you.

Amaya asks if the homeless woman knows how to swim.
This is the year scientists report coral larvae (coral, sea
anemones, jellyfish) respond to sound.

Kubisch wants everyone to hear the light.

Scientists don't want us to fall out of the sky.

I'm paralyzed in decision making. I don't want to decide
if we should leave.

They're trying to follow the movement of coral larvae.
Where do they disappear.

Where did she disappear.

I'm trying to figure out the point at which two dissimi-
lar objects collide. What is it that holds them together.
What is it that makes them fall apart.

NOT TO BURST
YOUR BUBBLE

It's been a month since Bret and I abandoned this space, and we have still have the keys. Technically, it's still our house because it hasn't been sold. The grass is overgrown, brown, and weeds sweep through the garden. My porch is empty. There are patches of uneven dirt where my mat and pots used to be.

I ring the doorbell like I'm a stranger to this place. I always loved this bell, a small silver circle enclosed in a rustic square. Most people had a hard time finding it or, when they did, they never pressed hard enough.

Next to the small doorbell is the mail slot attached to our house, which meant the mail carrier had to deliver the mail from door to door. This was one of my favorite things about the house. I had gotten used to the mailman consistently dropping our mail through the slot at approximately 2:45 pm each day. Our dog knew his arrival time by heart and waited at the edge of the slot, ready to bark the minute the mail was dropped. I grew comfortable in these consistencies.

This house was built in 1947, so there were many unique aspects that no longer exist in many newer developed homes.

Such as: the attached mailbox. As early as the 1880s, the U.S. Post Office began encouraging homeowners to attach wall-mounted mailboxes to the outside of their houses in place of mail slots, which didn't entail the mail carrier bending down, taking more time, more effort. Many of these early metal letter drops contained the word "LETTERS" across their small rectangular frames. This is beautiful and sad. I think of the handwritten letters collected in these boxes, stunning ink-blotted words written in cursive letters, carefully, line by line, detailing the day's events, the weather, the recipient reading these words, imagining these events as they unfold in their hands, tracing their fingers across the ink, time and space collapsing into that room.

The issue was time consumption. The goal: to get the mail delivered expediently. Some homes had large front yards to walk through. It was proposed that individual mail boxes for residential or business customers be mounted curbside on fence-posts, lamp-posts, or other supports, making it easier for the mail carrier to deliver box to box, not bending, not talking, his body working like a machine.

I remember when we first viewed this house in 2005. We were twenty-four/twenty-five, on the verge of marriage, on the verge of pregnancy, but didn't know it yet; the economy was on the verge of collapse and didn't know it yet. All we knew was we wanted a home, a place of our own. In the years before, we lived as apartment managers in a small complex. We grew tired of restless tenants, the constant knocking on our door, the invasions of our privacy, so we obsessively searched for a house to buy. But houses were being swept up as fast as they went up for sale in those days. We liked a house, got excited about it, we got outbid.

We became exhausted with the process. Bret liked one place. I hated it. Vice versa. When we stumbled into this house after driving around on a Sunday, it felt too good to be true. I loved the outside, the red door, the Tudor style. It reminded me of an old chapel. We opened the back gate and stepped into green, vines roped across the lot and house, wrapping around the fence like beautiful music notes. There was an old deck enclosing an overgrown Mulberry tree that unfolded into sky. It felt peaceful, like something sacred. It offered stability, what I needed. Before we even stepped inside, we called our realtor and told him if it was still available, we wanted it. We wanted to bid.

We didn't know the "housing bubble" was about to burst.

Or maybe we did. Relatives who told us to wait to buy warned us we were paying way too much for this house. I'll be the first to admit I wasn't thinking too far into the future, that we were also living in our own bubble, our need for immediate gratification, not thinking outside what we needed at that moment. In those beginning days, it felt like we were in a sort of romantic cocoon, unaware of the devastation imploding inside neighboring houses, people unable to afford their mortgages, on the verge of foreclosure.

Housing bubbles can happen in local or global real estate markets. In late stages, they're typically characterized by rapid increases in the appraisals of real property until unsound levels are reached relative to incomes, price to rent ratios, and other economic signs of affordability. This may be followed by decreases in home prices resulting in many owners finding themselves in a position of negative equity—a mortgage debt higher than the value of the property.

In other words, five years after buying it, we were $80,000 upside down.

We called our house a starter house, a fixer upper. We knew there were many projects to be done, but we didn't plan on staying for longer than ten years. We adopted a dog first. We refinished the hardwood floors. Bret dug trenches to install a new sprinkler system in the front and backyard. We planted four red Japanese maples in the front. We were immersed in it, in us.

There was much speculation, blame, and disagreement about whether or not there could be a "housing bubble," particularly at its peak from 2004-2006, with some rejecting the "housing bubble" label altogether.

Of course, now that I think back, maybe it was just me that ignored the signs. Bret was always more grounded, more financially responsible than I was. I remember him having reservations about the price of the place and the location and whether or not it was a good investment. But I loved it. I was too far inside the house, imagining our lives here. It all seemed risky, romantic.

In April of 2005, *The Economist* published an article stating: "The total value of residential property in developed economies rose by more than $30 trillion over the past five years, to over $70 trillion, an increase equivalent to 100% of those countries' combined GDPs. Not only does this dwarf any previous house-price boom, it is larger than the global stock market bubble in the late 1990s . . . in other words, it looks like the biggest bubble in history."

At this very same time, I took six pregnancy tests within two days to confirm whether or not I was pregnant. I had been drinking wine at a girlfriend's and casually mentioned to my friends I felt bloated, on the verge of my period, but that it wouldn't come. I was four days late. They urged me to take a test, but I waited for Bret to pick me up. I doubted I was and laughed about picking up a test that night at Long's Drug store, while we were en-route to meet our friends at a dive bar called Jimbo's. Bret seemed more concerned, insisting I take it that night. After much deliberation, I decided I would run into the Carl's Junior bathroom and settle this. I remember staring at the two emerging pale pink lines, rechecking the instructions a million times. Two lines = positive. I was afraid of what was to come. He cried joyful tears and told me everything was going to work out, that this was meant to be. I never imagined myself as a mother. I didn't quite know how to hold myself together, yet alone a child. The years were compressing into a whirlwind, and I still felt like I was running inside it all, aimlessly.

In the weeks we spent packing up this house, I remember finding the pregnancy test and reexamining it. I was holding it in another time, another light, not looking back but looking in. The two pink lines were still there, though now they seemed paler, faded, blurred at the edges. It's funny how you never know what's unfolding around you when you're inside it. Or maybe you do. When I think back now, I had all the normal pregnancy symptoms: enlarged and tender breasts, nausea, and exhaustion. I subconsciously ignored them.

In mid 2005, the then Federal Reserve Board Chairman Alan Greenspan said, "At a minimum, there's a little 'froth' (in the U.S. housing market) . . . it's hard not to see that there are a lot of local bubbles." In 2007, he admitted that *froth* was a "euphemism for a bubble."

I open the door and step inside our living/dining room. It seems different now that we're gone. There are black streaks on the walls from moving furniture, crayon marks from the kids. I trace my finger across the paint, remembering the day we spent painting this room. It seemed small at first but then the room expanded the farther we went along. We grew tired after painting and drinking well into the night, stumbling off to bed, laughing, covered in paint. We didn't have kids then. The house was ours, open and empty of constant sound.

I walk across the hardwood floors, examining the scratches and marks from six years of us. Then there are the unmarked areas that seem bare, exposed like the skin on a stomach, soft and new. We called our house a black hole because items disappeared. I remember how after the movers lifted the sofas, we found years of lost objects: pacifiers, dolls, books, crayons, spoons, and mail. Here they were back in our hands, resurfaced, returned to us after years of being gone. I held them close, trying to restore the histories attached to them.

It was harder for me to let go of the house. Bret was the one who studied the numbers. It was clear-cut to him: a bad investment. A psychologist told me it was harder for women to walk away from homes because we had emotional connections. It held memories of our family and stories. Us. It meant closing the door on these histories.

Although, now, the loss is clear to me as well: walking away from this space meant walking away from six years of us. At the time, I didn't know what walking away meant. I placed our house into the larger pool of loss, already swimming inside me and it frightened me.

I walk through each abandoned room, scanning each gap for forgotten items. The floors are dusty, clumps of hair are piled in corners. Other than that, to an observer, it would seem the people inside here vanished with all their belongings.

ROOM TO ROAM

> "The days divided into two: working and mothering. The third part, which is me, lives in my dreams."
>
> —Carmen Gimenez Smith

This morning I read about Isabela, a six-year-old girl, who vanished in the night from her bedroom in Tucson, Arizona. An open window, screen bent.

I dream I hear a window opening. In my dream, I rush into Amaya's room. I see an open window, black sky, big moon. I hear her but can't see her. I scream, fall to knees. Wake up.

3 am: I check, recheck, all windows. In our new house, we have thirty-eight. Recently walking away from our other house, it feels like a form of molting—shedding ourselves from an exoskeleton—only to move into another. The other house was left behind, like a deserted casing of bones.

Amaya has four windows in her bedroom. I watch her sleep, pull her hair away from her eyes. Did I tell her I loved her enough before she went to bed? I wished her to sleep in a selfish rush. I wanted to be alone, to read. After she went to sleep, I felt guilty that I was a terrible mother.

To be a mother is to never be alone, even in the most secluded space.

We moved into a house twenty miles outside of town. It's ranch style and sits on fifteen acres of almond trees. It's the best of both worlds. Built in 1948, it has all the old charm and eccentricity I love, but it's also restored, every nook and cranny has been renovated, so it offers the new appeal that Bret loves. Our yard is vast space, dusty sky, massive trees. Lots of mud. It feels like a retreat in the sense we're away from everything. We searched for houses in the country, so the kids could have room to roam, to be kids. We also subconsciously needed it for us. We needed another beginning.

I have a hard time being present. I get distracted easily. My mind wanders. I feel guilty during the times I spend away in my head while with my kids, thinking of floating ideas I want to write about. Lately, I'm trying to absorb the space with them, to really be part of their world, to see the way they see, in the moment, in the new.

This week, I'm using my nondominant hand for ordinary tasks as part of a mindful exercise within the book *How To Train A Wild Elephant*. These exercises attempt to bring us back to what Zen teachers call, "the beginner's mind." It's a task that asks you to relearn what you know. To undo what you know and start over. I feel ridiculously awkward. I've never had the patience for meditation.

I ask Amaya to do this with me. We laugh at our clumsiness. Our left arms feel rigid as we try to brush our teeth with them. She says it's too hard to eat left handed because she can't hold her wrist still. To start again is an attempt to learn to balance again, to reshape our habits. In its most basic element, it's an attempt to learn to live again. For someone with major anxiety, which manifests itself in drastic attempts to control the environment, this is incredibly difficult. It means surrendering, which is a terrifying word to me.

Things in the country are new to me: long gopher snakes slither through grass. The first time I see one, I scream and fall backward like a bewildered child. I watch it slide through grass back into his hole. I learn they are good for the garden and are harmless, keeping the rodents out, so I keep my distance. Many mornings, I find pieces of dead mice on my porch, a head here, a tail over there. I pick the pieces up with a shovel and drop them into snake holes with my eyes closed.

Like all snakes, gopher snakes shed the outermost layer of skin as they begin to grow. The new skin, beneath the outer layer, is newer, more vibrant. This process is called "ecdysis," which is from Ancient Greek—*ekduo*—or to take off, strip off.

Even the air out in the country is new. It's dusty, dry. My kids turn the hose on and make mud lakes throughout our yard. They swim, sliding through it. At night, the sky flickers with bright stars. I relearn the constellations, rediscovering this love of following patterns, connecting the dots. Bret surprises me with a telescope for Mother's Day and we enjoy the starry nights in our backyard, outside the city, relearning us.

Recently, scientists announced the discovery of a particle they believed to behave in the same manor of the Higgs boson. Media outlets called it "God's particle." Although I had to do much research, to go back to the basics to understand the magnitude of this study, I was submerged in the language, captured by the mystery, indulging in the wonder. I was lost in the language of the cosmos: photons, neutrons, electrons, quarks and leptons, forces that act upon matter and the most intriguing of all, the boson, a particle, which physicists have described as "weights anchored by mysterious rubber bands to the matter particles that generate them. Using this analogy, we can think of the particles constantly snapping back out of existence in an instant and yet equally capable of getting entangled with other rubber bands attached to other bosons (and imparting force in the process)." Imagine the minds and emotions of the scientists, who have unraveled a timeless mystery, while working with the Large Haldron Collider, molding an idea and theory that had baffled and intrigued minds for years—the piece to this puzzle—this boson, which is responsible for all the mass in the universe.

As we unravel a new piece to the larger puzzle, it opens the door to another mystery, to more questions, more wonder. What's incredible is how the mind and imagination can stretch like a rubber band, extending into unknown territory, disappearing briefly, yet bouncing back into the present.

Some days at home are incredibly long. The hours move like a slug across pavement, and I want to escape. I get anxious. Bored. I don't want to jump on the trampoline one more time. Or play dress up. Or clean up spilled cheerios. Or wipe up mud that was tracked inside.

I grow skeptical of the implication of the title—*How To Train A Wild Elephant.* Why would a wild elephant need to be trained? I think of the beauty of raw emotions, how elephants mourn their dead with delicate care and deep sadness, the way they stay close to the bones of their lost loved ones, touching the bones with tusks.

Henry David Thoreau: "The most alive is the wildest."

Without mass, we would fly through the universe, traveling at the speed of light.

On long days, I turn on my music. Cash. The Boss. Patti Smith. Stevie Nicks. *It's loooud,* my two-year-old says, covering his ears. I tell him it's good for him. To get rhythm. He shakes his booty for a bit with me before wandering off to play in the other room with his sister. I hear them fight. Someone falls. I turn my music up. I tell myself in order for them to thrive they also need to play alone, to use their imaginations. I tell myself this to make myself feel less guilty. Because I'm often caught between dueling convictions: I want to mother and be something other.

Escapism is a mental diversion by means of entertainment or recreation. As in: an escape from the banal facets of daily life. It can also be used to define the actions people take to relieve persisting feelings of sadness.

My good-mom friend tells me if she doesn't go back to work soon, she'll go insane, have a breakdown. What is it like to go insane? Is that to disappear too far? There must be a line somewhere.

Dad worked long hours when I was young, like Bret does now. When he returned from work, my mom grabbed his keys. She didn't have a car, and she had four kids. We all chased behind her, tugging her leg, asking, "Where are you going, Mommy? Where are you going?" She always said, "Crazy, I'm going crazy." We all told her we wanted to go too. Whenever I'm hard on myself, Mom always shares this story and we laugh about it again and again.

What's so wrong with entering the emotions we fear?

My kids never call me "Mother." They call me Mom or Mama or Mommy. Sometimes, Anderson imitates Bret and calls me, "Liz" or "Liz-a-bedth." We laugh at his cuteness. I ask Amaya what a mother is. She says, "A mother is a mammal." I ask her what a human mother is. She tells me human mothers are mommies with soft hands.

Before Amaya was born, I never imagined myself as a "mother." My older sister was a mother of two—a three-and-a-half-old and a three-month-old at the time of her death. I remember telling her when she was pregnant with her second she would have all the kids for me. It's been more than ten years since I watched her walk out her front door the day she was killed in a car accident four minutes from her house. I spent most of these years trying to recreate her.

These days, I feel flashes of profound happiness. I feel guilty for releasing the grief. Even in moments of joy, I feel hints of sadness. Or maybe it's guilt. Can happiness exist alongside tragedy?

Recently I read that investigators reopened the case of Etan Patz, a six-year-old boy who disappeared on May 25, 1979—the year I was born. He vanished on his two-block walk to the bus stop. I think of the agony of the parents, who must relive this day, or his last seconds a million times. It was the first time they ever let him walk to the bus stop alone. Etan was the first child to be featured on a milk carton. I see his face, slanted smile, and I think of my son. I think of my childhood, of growing up, living the years he missed.

I think of how many times I've disappeared on the computer, turned my head away for seconds, minutes. Someone could have _____.

Police say it's incredibly rare for a child to be abducted from his or her bedroom. 25% of kids are taken by strangers.

My mother used to always tell us a story of two girls who were riding banana bikes home from school when a stranger snatched one of them, sealed her into a trunk, while the other escaped. How does someone escape from that?

I try not to write about my kids. I want to avoid sentimentality. Somehow, everything I do and write about is filtered through them. Whenever I try to write as something other, the other becomes the mother and the mother becomes the other.

I overextend. I underextend.

I've tried to blame the guilt on my Catholic upbringing.

Where do these pressures/prescriptions come from?

In my class, we discuss John Berger's *Ways Of Seeing*. He argues that "we see first," we learn language after, but it becomes a dynamic relationship later because what we see is largely influenced by our assumptions, what we've learned through language.

To code switch is to talk in different language styles among groups. For example, I tell my students, I talk in fragments with my kids. In class, I talk in long circular sentences.

Mother Tongue is the language a person has learned since birth. The mother sharpens the linguistic skills of a child. As in: the language spoken by the mother would be the primary language the child learns.

I learned to mother from my mother from her mother from her mother from what mothers I've observed from what I've been told is expected of mothers from men who also had mothers. But I wasn't born a mother.

Maybe this is because I entered by accident. I became a mother before I learned how to mother. I suppose the only way to learn to mother is to become one. I felt unprepared for the invasion of privacy, the intrusion of stethoscopes and Doppler's and fingers and ideals. I was unprepared for the pain of each contraction during labor when the epidural failed. The pain was intense, unbearable. I cussed in a Catholic hospital. I squeezed Bret's hand. He looked more afraid than I was, unable to know what I was experiencing inside, which frustrated him. I focused on the blue ceiling lights and my mom, who kept reappearing to bless me and pray over me in a low voice I recognized from childhood. Nobody ever told me this also hurt like hell. But I learned women were taught to just bear it.

I remember seeing Amaya during those brief blurry seconds and remarking that she looked like my sister, her rosy skin and strawberry blonde hair. We called her "Rosebud," nicknamed from her middle name, Rose, which was also my sister's middle name.

When you lose someone suddenly, it takes a while to absorb their absence, to understand they're not going to walk back through the door, and the sadness comes in waves, unexpectedly. Some days are worse than others.

I don't feel like I fit in with mothers at parks: the ones with huge diaper bags with a gazillion pockets with a gazillion snacks and teething toys. I always feel unprepared.

I've been stuck in this penumbral space between where I'm still trying to hold on to my other self and also be a mother at the same time.

Amaya calls our new home the "house that never loses anything." She's determined never to lose any of her items this time around. I'm also vigilant in her quest and have echoed this will be the house where nothing gets lost.

Etan Patz's parents still live in the same apartment they lived in the day he vanished. They have the same phone number, in the event he may return, try to contact them. As I write this, I've learned they have a suspect in custody, who has confessed to killing the boy. My eyes close. I don't want to hear the how. I think of his parents, thirty-three years later, still waiting for him to come home.

I don't consider my grief in my sister's loss to be greater than anyone else's. In fact, at times, I feel guilty for my sadness when I'm aware of all the tragedies in the world and mine feels small in comparison. I have a hard time reconciling that because even knowing this, I can't escape the hurt. I recognize how unprepared I was, how even at times, ten years later, I collapse in tears at some sudden memory or image of her. Just the other day, as I was slipping into a pair of sandals, and the way the air entered the arch on my narrow foot reminded me of her and her feet, her arch. Did we ever talk about this? I couldn't remember.

I was twenty-five when I became pregnant with Amaya, a year older than my sister when she died. I remember that year being tough, surreal and hard to navigate because I didn't want to move forward. I didn't want to pass my big sister in age. It was also three years after her death. Everything felt heavy, watered.

In the early days after Amaya was born, my twenty-sixth birthday seemed to slip by unnoticed. Everything seemed foggy, disconnected from my spot on the sofa, where I nursed for hours a day, disappearing in time and space.

Family members remarked my sister had some hand in the gender of my child, that it was no coincidence that she was as fair-skinned and rosy as she was. I felt comfort in this, and even more vigilant in my attempt to protect her.

I loved Amaya's small body, attached to mine, so vulnerable and dependent. With this intense love came an intense fear: I couldn't survive without her. Our relationship became symbiotic: I needed her and she needed me.

I realize now I'm more afraid of outliving all my loved ones than I am of dying. Although both of these are terrifying, the first has a little more edge to it.

Most people say their second pregnancies are easier. They know what to expect, so they just roll through the stages. For me it was the opposite, since I knew what to expect, I knew the massive amount of love and fear that was going to overtake, overpower, overwhelm me. I knew I couldn't ever go back.

Adrienne Rich: "Re-vision—the act of looking back, of seeing with fresh eyes, of entering an old text from a new critical direction—is for woman more than a chapter in cultural history: it is an act of survival. Until we understand the assumptions in which we are drenched we cannot know ourselves." I attempt to redefine myself in my new house, in my new garden, my new vegetables. I see new growth. Possibility. Beauty. Relationships. Bret. I marvel at a hummingbird nest nearby, at the eggs. I tend my garden daily, pulling weeds, ensuring survival.

A few weeks after we move in, I am consumed with another sudden disappearance. A teenage girl in northern California disappeared in early morning on her walk to her bus stop. A month after her disappearance, authorities arrest a man, who lived in a city nearby, who was possibly just driving through the area on his hunt for a job. He was connected to the case by traces of his DNA found on her duffle bag that was tossed in a nearby field. I see striking similarities between the rural area in which she lived and my new town. By her, there were vast golden fields, arcing hills. Here by me, streets stretch through vast orchards and curling vineyards.

On my drive to and from work, I imagine her walking toward a stop sign. I see a suspicious car and I try to cut him off, divert and stall him, so her school bus will arrive before he has a chance to snatch her. I do this obsessively. I'm enraged with her abductor, accused killer. I see myself as her, getting into his car that morning. I punch at him, claw him, kick, scream. I'm overtaken with rage. I'm fighting for her life.

Anne Carson: "Why does tragedy exist? Because you are full of rage. Why are you full of rage? Because you are full of grief."

"What is this about?" my therapist asks. "I want them all to return," I say. "Yes," she says, "and what else?" And as illogical and silly as it sounds coming out of my mouth, I say it anyway. "Because I want to save them." She nods and waits. "Because I couldn't save my sister." I feel the lump in my throat lessen, my fists uncurl.

I'm so afraid of loss I'm afraid to live, to love, of not loving enough, of loving too much. The threat of loss always overshadows all else, pulling me in, so in a sense I'm never fully present, and I feel so incredibly guilty.

I've tried to etch together a blueprint, a map to navigate loss and motherhood, a pamphlet for survival, but the truth is: there's no such thing. That would be too predictable. When I was small, I used to spin the globe with my finger pressed into one spot with my eyes closed, and when it stopped I was supposed to read the place where my finger had pressed and that would be the place I lived as an adult. Most of the time I ended up in the middle of the ocean—vast blue space. There's so much that can't be explained. But the beauty is before the discovery, the moments spent wandering, exploring, getting lost. This is the wild.

I'm vulnerable, limited, exposed, unprepared. I fail and will fail again and again. But I keep going because with each failure there's another beginning. Again and again.

When I leave, I kiss my kids on their foreheads and tell them, "I'll be back soon." It's not really a lie. It's a slanted truth. Even language is limited. I always plan to return. But no one can say with certainty.

In "Walking," Thoreau describes the outline which bordered his walks as a "parabola, or rather like one of those cometary orbits which would have been thought to be non-returning curves. . . ." Parabolas can open up, down, left, right or in some other random direction. They are all similar, and even though they can be different sizes, they are all the same shape. A parabola can also be attained as the limit of a sequence of ellipses where one focus is kept fixed as the other is allowed to move randomly far away in one direction, which means a parabola may be considered an ellipse that has one focus at infinity.

Just the other night, while tucking Amaya into bed, she said, "Do you know how far I love you, Mommy?" I told her to give me a hint. "All the way to the planet that disappeared." I searched her face for more information. "To Pluto, Mom. Because that was my favorite planet, and it disappeared." That's where I want to imagine my sister and all the others, on a planet that was, then wasn't, a gray spot, spinning among infinite stars within an unmapped sky.

NOTES

ON "WHAT IS THE SHAPE"

One day, I was in my kitchen, emptying out a junk drawer and came across a strange shaped spoon. It wasn't a ladle, but it looked similar. I pondered its shape for several minutes, trying to recall its origins. I realized it was part of a set I had inherited from my sister before she died. Most of the other pieces to that set were gone, misplaced. For days, I obsessed over shapes: grief, anger, loss, and things I couldn't find words for.

During this time, I thought of George Kubler's book, *The Shape of Time: Remarks on the History of Things,* published by Yale University in 1962, which I mention in this essay.

ON "THE END OF A WORLD AS WE KNOW IT"

"It's the End of the World as We Know It (And I Feel Fine)" is a song by the rock band R.E.M., which first appeared on their 1987 album, *Document.* The title of this essay was borrowed from this song. As I was re-searching this essay, I came across so many articles in which many people associated the demotion of Pluto as the sign of the end days, so it reminded me of this song, which has always been one of my favorites.

I never intended to write an essay about Pluto, but that's the amazing beauty of writing and reading. It gives you the license to explore, to let your mind wander, and to lose yourself in language. After a couple of weeks of im-mersing myself in articles about Pluto and its demotion, I became fascinated with the scientific language. The words and facts and stories and opinions were allur-ing. I read and reread everything on the NASA website, which is where many of the facts are pulled from. I also read several journal articles during this time, submerg-ing myself in this language. These articles included, "Clyde Tombaugh," *Astronomy & Space: From the Big Bang to the Big Crunch,* published in 2008; "More Than a One-Hit Wonder," *Astronomy, Volume 4, Number 2,* published in 2006; "Pluto and Charon," *Earth Sciences For Students,* published in 2008. I also pulled a lot of the facts from *The Gale Encyclopedia of Science* (2010).

The essay then became more of an exploration into the unknown, into language and loss. As I wrote, the pat-terns and other associations surfaced. In my graduate student days, I read a lot of William Carlos Williams, who said, "No ideas but in things." I was also thinking a lot about consciousness, and how we use language to make sense of the world, so this naturally led me to Helen Keller, who wrote, "When I learned the meaning of 'I' and 'me' and found that I was something, I began to think. Then consciousness first existed for me" in her book, *The World I Live In,* first published by The Century Co. in 1908. This led me to Thomas Hobbes's, *Leviathan,* first published by Oxford: Clarendon Press in 1651. In many ways, this essay was an investigation into unraveling the complexity of ways of knowing, so I was also wondering about the ways the mind moves. In a poetry class I took in graduate school, the professor taught us to move associatively, to think in a "stream of consciousness," which comes from William James's article, "The Stream Of Consciousness," first published in *Psychology* in 1892.

ON "TEN YEARS AFTER"

In grief, the ten-year anniversary is supposed to be rough. You know this ahead of time because people remind you that it will be an emotional train wreck. But the truth is, most days following the death of a loved one blur into one massive collision. There are some days that crush you more than others out of nowhere. So in the month leading up to her anniversary, I had been thinking I was going to be fine because I had convinced myself that it was just going to be another day. In actuality, the entire weekend destroyed me all over again. I wasn't prepared for that, like I wasn't prepared for her accident.

This is (arguably) one of the most emotional essays in the book. I wrote this essay the day after I visited her grave. I wanted to get as close to the grief as possible because I was also trying to make sense of it myself.

Often times, it's assumed that writers pour their emotions onto the page. For me, most of the time, it's the opposite. I pound into the keyboard and then after I read what I've written, I experience the emotions. I wanted this essay to be raw, so I wrote it in one day, and only revised it once before sending it off to Juked where it was published the next month. It has received very little revisions since then.

ON "IT BEGINS"

Parts of this essay were originally poems I had been working on in grad school. They weren't working on their own, but I didn't want to part with them because they kept haunting me.

Also, this essay was originally titled, "It Begins in Neon Lights."

I wanted to recreate the feeling of being haunted, so I decided that many of these poems could be put into a collage form in which they were working with and against one another. I wanted it to have a similar effect as a flashback.

During the time of writing this, I had also been reading *Our Babies, Ourselves: How Biology and Culture Shape the Way We Parent,* written by Meredith Smalls. A friend gave me this book after my daughter was born and I'm constantly revisiting it. I thought about biology and brains a lot during the infant years. I was always worried. I was always obsessing. I rarely slept. I read a lot. Sometimes, the words I was reading appeared in dreams. I wanted to show how we slip into other voices and realms simultaneously and the collage form was the only way to attempt to mirror that.

ON "JELLYFISH"

Jellyfish are gorgeous and brilliant creatures. While writing this essay, I was thinking about paleontology because I was reading Neil Shubin's, *Your Inner Fish: A Journey into the 3.5-Billion-Year History of the Human Body,* published in January 2009. I was also worrying about kidnappings and pedophiles because they seemed to be flooding the media.

As I read this book, I began noticing patterns during quiet moments with Amaya. We visited the Monterey Aquarium. I fell in love with jellyfish. Shubin also writes, "We were not designed rationally, but are products of a convoluted history." I began paying attention to the interconnectivity of things of this world, exploring the spaces. Having kids also forces you to look closer at things, and since I was open to it, my senses were overwhelmed with seeing connections in language and detail between humans and animals.

In the essay, I refer to a child, who was kidnapped. Although during the space of writing this, there were several kidnappings, so the child mentioned in this essay was an amalgam of many cases that I had been seeing on the news.

All of this was on my mind and all of this was overlapping. I wanted to recreate this overlapping and explore these tensions on the page. I wanted all of these disparate elements to smash into one another in an attempt to speak to and against one another. I'm always interested in collisions and in the space before collisions.

ON "LOCKDOWN"

I wrote this prose poem immediately following a lockdown at my daughter's school. She was in kindergarten at the time. Strangely and unnervingly enough, it was written before Sandy Hook. After the Sandy Hook massacre, I thought about adding that into the essay, but I felt like it would have changed the meaning of the moment. I wanted to reinvent the sense of urgency and desperation and insanity that I felt in that moment. This is important because I think there's a tendency to move forward quickly in our culture, especially with grief. I wanted to get this out. Fear and panic isn't something that's talked about much between mothers at parks or elsewhere.

ON "DOOR COLLECTING"

For a long time, I was obsessed with doors, especially old doors. I saw them as openings/closings, where we could slip into new worlds, histories, dreams, voices, and close the door on those we didn't want to enter. I photographed doors I loved. I placed my kids in front of some. The doorknobs felt like strange hands.

This essay did begin with a man, who sold old doors. Every Sunday, I passed by his house, where he lined them up in his lawn. Mostly, he had old ones with missing hinges or knobs. I thought it was so beautiful to see them on display in his lawn. Finally, I stopped one Sunday and asked him about the doors and how he obtained them. He said he had also been infatuated with doors, that he found them in alleys sometimes or in dumpsters behind department stores. I began thinking about collecting and why we have this urge to collect certain objects. Writing in so many ways overlaps with psychology and anthropology and ethnography, among other things. I began writing and researching, and the door became a sort of metaphor for this. For each question I asked, it was like opening another door into another idea or history or story.

The man who sold the doors told me that no two were the same, and somehow this spiraled into sporadic research on snowflakes. Most of the information pertaining to snowflakes came from the research I collected from the database SIRS. I entered "snowflakes and obsessions" into the search field and went from there. The whole process moved associatively, where I just let my mind wander from one thing to the next. The articles I referenced most pertaining to Wilson A. Bentley and the science behind the snowflakes were, "In Praise of Snow," published by *Atlantic Monthly* in January 1995 and "What You Need To Know About Snow," published by *Philadelphia Inquirer* in January 2003.

I'm always collecting facts and various objects. I wanted the form to mirror this. I stumbled upon Marjorie

Akin's article, "Passionate Possession: The Formation of Private Collections," from *Learning from Things: Method and Theory of Material Cultural Studies* published by Smithsonian Institution Press in 1996. I was reminded of how messy the world is and how messy our minds are. Collecting objects and collecting facts seemed to be an attempt at creating order, even though reality is so much messier than that, but the more I wrote this essay, the more I realized how much we try to make sense of disorder, which made me think of a Wallace Stevens' poem, "Connoisseur of Chaos."

I began collecting facts about the heart and electrocardiograms. I searched through databases, dissecting and absorbing the details. I pulled many facts from *The Gale Encyclopedia of Science* and from the journal, *Gale Science In Context*.

When I told a friend about how I was writing about snow, he led me to *The Six-Cornered Snowflake* by Johannes Kepler, which I referenced in the essay.

In many ways, I felt like I was piecing a puzzle together with words, which reminded me of Lewis Carroll's, *Through the Looking Glass.*

ON "SO MUCH DEPENDS UPON A CREDENZA"

This essay was a compilation of fragments of ideas and images that I had been thinking about for months. One day, I started thinking of them together and realized how much they spoke to one another in interesting ways.

It did begin with the credenza, which became the metaphor for the seemingly degradation of my life at the time.

I love watching and exploring how things in this world overlap and intersect, especially with science.

Also, parts of this essay came to me while being stuck at Albany International Airport for several hours. Airports in general are amazing places. People are in this transitory state. Everyone is on the go. Time feels very heavy and weighted here, even though, it's such a temporary space. I walked all about the airport, examining the wall art and came across the Clocktower Project by Christina Kubisch. The way this beautiful old clock was able to expand and collapse time was fascinating, especially seeing photos on display in the airport, where people are both moving away from and behind time. I wrote down fragments of information that I found in the airport about it, and I followed up with doing my own research, gathering most from the Massachusetts Museum of Contemporary Art's website, http://www.massmoca.org.

I love science, and I love reading science news. It's always on my mind, so most of the time these facts make their way into the backdrop of my essays. In this essay, most of the facts came from "Light Can Generate Lift" by Laura Sanders, published in *Science News,* January 2011 and "Young'uns Adrift On The Sea" by Susan Milius, published in *Science News,* January 2011.

ON "NOT TO BURST YOUR BUBBLE"

For the research of this essay, I did a massive Internet search of "housing bubble." I was in the middle of walking away from my house, and it occurred to me how very little I understood the housing market collapse. As I read various articles, mostly from *The Economist*, the similarities in the language used to describe housing bubbles struck me as being so similar to the collapse of so many other things, so this was used as a window or a lens to look inside the language of downfall.

ON "ROOM TO ROAM"

I wrote much of this essay after reading Carmen Gimenez Smith's, *Bring Down The Little Birds*. I was so inspired by the fragmented form, and the ways in which the form mirrors the mindset of the speaker. I was also relieved to finally read a gut-wrenchingly honest book about motherhood.

I was also on a quest to live more peacefully. I was in therapy, and my therapist recommended several meditation books that I read and absorbed during this period, such as: *How To Train a Wild Elephant*, by Jan Chozen, and *Something More*, by Sarah Ban Breathnach. Normally, I have a strong aversion to self-helpy type books because of their tendency to use overly fluffy language and to simplify complex things, but these offered more tactile solutions. However, I did grow frustrated midway through my quest for peace and returned to my skeptical and anxious self. As I became frustrated, I thought a lot about Henry David Thoreau, so I pulled out a copy of *Walking*. I referenced this thin book, which very much reads like a prose poem or an essay on life. In many ways, it's better than any self-help book. While reading this, I wanted to just saunter in the woods.

The Higgs boson news was also everywhere at this time, which of course was a welcoming distraction. I ate up the news and informational articles pertaining to this. Much of the research for this came from the website, science.howstuffworks.com.

This essay is also about perception and how we came to what we know. I was reading John Berger's, *Ways of Seeing* during this period and I was also teaching him to my students.

I read a lot of Adrienne Rich during my graduate years, and I reread her words many times. When I became a mother, I thought a lot about *Of Women Born*, and all the unconventional and honest ways, she wrote about motherhood.

I've also read many books about grief and loss. Most of them, I don't enjoy because of how few can actually get inside what it means to grieve. In graduate school, I was introduced to Anne Carson, who is still one of my favorite writers. In this essay, I referenced her book, *Grief Lessons: Four Plays.*

Liz Scheid holds an MFA (poetry) from California State University, Fresno. She teaches English composition classes at Fresno City College. Her essays and poems have appeared in several literary magazines, including, *The Rumpus, Mississippi Review, Third Coast, Sou'Wester, The Journal, The Collagist, Terrain, and others*. Her work has been nominated for a Pushcart Prize twice. She currently lives in an almond orchard in Kerman, California with her husband and their two wonderful kids.